PRAY
Like It
Matters

STEVE GAINES, PH.D.
FOREWORD BY JOHNNY HUNT

Auxano
PRESS

ISBN 978-0-9889854-2-1

Published by Auxano Press
Tigerville, South Carolina
www.AuxanoPress.com

Printed in the United States of America
22 21 20 19—12 11 10 9 8

I dedicate this book to
Brother Don Miller
of Fort Worth, Texas,
the most humble,
Christlike man of prayer
I have ever known.
He taught me to pray and sing:
"Down on my knees,
Down on my knees,
All things are possible
Down on my knees!"

Contents

Foreword

Every now and then we take a book in our hands and begin to read its cover and introductory remarks only to find that we can't think of a deeper matter in our heart as it pertains to our own personal life, the church that we are a part of, or that we pastor than what we are about to read. I feel confident that most people who read this book will share that they have a desire that needs to meet with a greater devotion in order to make a greater impact and difference in their life, the circumstances around them, the life of the church that they lead, and even the Kingdom and its God that they serve.

Dr. Steve Gaines has done us a great favor in writing *Pray Like It Matters*. All of us would say that prayer does make a difference and that it really matters; but, if you are like me, many times I spend more time planning to pray than praying the plan that God has placed before me. As you walk through the simple chapters of this book, it is my prayer that God will do in both your life and mine a fresh work of seeing prayer become a major priority. For years now, I have practiced giving a minimum of an hour every morning to prayer and devotion, but this book has reminded me that most of my devotion is reading instead of praying and talking to God; and, even when I find myself praying, it is more of me talking and it being a one-sided conversation instead of me allowing God to speak back into my life. I am grateful to be challenged afresh and anew that I not only need to give some time in the morning to the Lord, but also realize that there are times when faced with important decisions that God will, indeed, call us to a prayer retreat where we will seek Him and not let go until we have heard clearly His decisive direction for our life. Who will ever pick up this book that will not need to know what to do when tempted? What better way to face temptation than to pray. When suffering comes in our lives in whatever way, be it persecution or challenges with health, we must pray because prayer matters.

I have known Dr. Steve Gaines to be a man of prayer, and have been personally touched by his prayer life. Not only has his interceding for me made a difference, but on one occasion in particular, when he laid hands on me and prayed, God instantly healed me. This is a day and moment in my life that I will never forget. When someone asks me about the life and person of Steve Gaines, I always readily say that I know him and that he is a man of God and a man of deep, devotional prayer. I believe that prayer is what has made the difference in the life of Steve Gaines; and it is not just true in his life, but also true in the life of his godly wife who has walked with him for so long. Both Donna and Steve are committed to a life of prayer.

I predict that as you start reading this book you will find it difficult to put it down. What a great joy it will be to walk through it in either a Bible study lesson, or one that you choose to read for your own personal edification. Remember, God will use prayer to shake us as well as shape us. May He shape each of us into people who genuinely believe that prayer really does matter. Read, and be blessed.

Johnny Hunt

INTRODUCTION

Do our prayers matter? Do they make a difference? I believe they do. They matter to God, to the circumstances and people around us, and to each of us as well. Things turn out differently when we pray than when we do not. God will do some things whether we pray or not. But there are some things God will do only if we pray. In many ways, our lives are the result of the prayers we've prayed as well as the ones we have not.

When I read the Book of Acts, I am embarrassed. Why does our brand of Christianity look so insipid compared to the believers of the First Century? Where has the power gone? Has God changed, or have we? We've all heard the cop out that says, "The Book of Acts represents a different dispensation." What a sad, self-serving attempt to excuse our current state of spiritual impotence!

When we read Acts, we should yearn to experience a return to their brand of Christianity. Yet, instead of copying them, we seem content with copying other modern churches that are "growing." But why copy a copy, when you can copy the original (the Book of Acts)? In Acts, God was saving people every day. Communities were transformed. People were healed. Demons were cast out. Miracles were commonplace. Churches sprouted up across the Roman Empire. Persecution was faced and overcome. What made them so different?

Some say they preached a purer Gospel. I disagree. Modern Evangelicals preach the same Gospel that was proclaimed in the First Century. We preach that Jesus was born of a virgin, lived a sinless life, died an atoning death, and rose bodily from the grave. We preach that man is a sinner and stands guilty before God in need of salvation. We preach that God offers salvation by grace, through faith, in Jesus Christ alone, and the moment anyone repents of his sin, puts his faith in Jesus, and calls upon His name, that person is born again. That's the Gospel they preached, and the Gospel we preach.

Our lack of spiritual power in Christianity today is not due to the sermons we preach or the songs we sing. Rather, it is due to our lack of prayer. We do not pray like it matters. Jesus and His earliest followers prayed like it was important. We pray like it is inconvenient or inconsequential. Prayer was their priority. It is our postscript. We plan more than we pray. They prayed more than they planned. We gather to minister to one another. They gathered to minister to the Lord in prayer and fasting. Our focus is earthly, horizontal. Theirs was heavenly, vertical. They were wise enough to "pray the price."

All of this is why I have written this 12-week Bible Study entitled, *"Pray Like It Matters."* I want to demonstrate from Scripture that every prayer we pray is significant. Through our prayers, God changes things. One life dedicated to prayer can do more good than any life dedicated to other so-called "noble," worldly causes. An individual follower of Jesus who is committed to prayer is a fountain of life in a world of death. Likewise, the local church that becomes a house of prayer will be a spiritual powerhouse from which God's mighty miracles will flow exponentially. PRAYER is what modern Christians and churches are missing - frequent, fervent, faithful prayer!

Most Christians want to pray but don't know how. They are unable to carry on a simple, sustained, satisfying conversation with God. Thus, after a few minutes in prayer, they run out of things to say, get frustrated, and give up. Sound familiar?

Just as infants must be taught to talk, Christians must be taught to pray. Once you know how, prayer will be fulfilling, refreshing, and even fun.

A growing number of Christians today are aware that something must be wrong. They know there has to be "more" to the Christian life than what they have experienced. That "more" is found through the discipline of prayer. These lessons are a wakeup call for each individual, family, and church to become a "house of prayer." When we begin to pray like Jesus and His early followers, then we will witness the power they experienced.

Today, we embark on what could be the greatest adventure of your life. Before we start, let's pray the prayer of the early disciples: **"Lord, teach us to pray"** (Luke 11:1).

If you meant that single-sentence prayer, buckle up your spiritual seatbelt. Your life is about to shift into high gear. God is about to take you places you have never been before!

III John 2,
Steve Gaines, Ph.D.
Bellevue Baptist Church
Memphis, TN
June 2013

The Priority of Prayer: The Prayer Life of Jesus

Mark 1:35 - "In the early morning, while it was still dark, Jesus got up, left the house, and went away to a secluded place, and was praying there."

No one ever prayed like Jesus. When it comes to prayer, He truly is the "expert." While on earth, Jesus prayed with a depth of intimacy that is unmatched. He communed with God through thanksgiving, petition, intercessions, and spiritual warfare. No one ever prayed like the Master.

When theologians discuss Jesus' life and ministry, they often focus on His insightful teachings, His compassion for the poor and needy, His mercy and grace toward sinners, His liberating power to heal the sick and cast out demons, and His uncanny ability to outsmart the Jewish religious leaders of His day who often opposed Him. Yet, these same theologians often fail to emphasize Jesus' prayer life. Reading the Gospels reveals how important prayer was to our Lord. You can transform your prayer life by studying Jesus' life and following His example in prayer.

Jesus Prayed in the Morning

Jesus set aside every morning for His Father. In Mark's Gospel we read about a busy day in His ministry. He taught in the synagogue, cast out a demon from a man in the audience, went to Peter's house, healed Peter's mother-in-law from a fever, dined with His disciples, healed many sick people, and cast out demons from those who flocked to Him in Capernaum. Yet, in spite of such a busy schedule, Jesus rose early the next morning to spend time alone with His Father in prayer.

Mark 1:35 says, "In the early morning, while it was still dark, Jesus got up, left the house, and went away to a secluded place, and was praying there." I like to point out that Jesus won "the battle of the covers!" Though He was no doubt tired, He got out of bed, left the house, went to a solitary place, and prayed!

For Christians, early mornings are primarily for prayer (cf. Ps. 5:3; 143:8), before we exercise, read the paper, or check emails. The Lord's Prayer itself is a morning prayer, otherwise, the phrase, "Give us this day our daily bread" (Matt. 6:11) makes little sense. Before we communicate with anyone else in the morning, we should talk with God.

Jesus Took Prayer Retreats

Jesus was busy, but He was never frantic or stressed out. Everywhere He went, He left a trail of tranquility. Why? Because everywhere He went, He prayed. He recognized the significance of building "spiritual margin" into His schedule. A bowstring loses its elasticity if it is always taut. Athletic teams take "time-outs" for a reason. Someone wisely said, "We should come apart before we come apart!" Taking time off from normal activities to commune with God is a surefire way to find true rest and renewal.

Luke 5:16 says, "But Jesus Himself would often slip away to the wilderness and pray." The phrase *slip away* is

special. It means that Jesus did this discreetly, not os-
tentatiously. He quietly slipped away and spent time in
prayer. Although He was God in the flesh, I believe these
frequent prayer retreats were one of the primary channels
God used to infuse Jesus with spiritual power for ministry.
We need those retreats as well.

Jesus Prayed before Making Important Decisions

In Luke 6, we read that Jesus healed a man who had
a withered hand. The healing took place on the Sabbath,
which greatly agitated the legalistic nerves of the Jewish
scribes and Pharisees. How did Jesus respond? Luke 6:12
says, "It was at this time that He went off to the mountain
to pray, and He spent the whole night in prayer to God."
The next morning, Jesus chose His twelve disciples. I believe there was a connection between His all-night prayer
meeting and the selection of those men. The Father
directed His decisions that night regarding whom He was
to choose.

What would happen in our churches if we prayed like
Jesus did before we make significant decisions about
choosing staff members, deacons, teachers, or other
leaders? The Lord would give us wisdom (James 1:5) and
direction (Ps. 32:8) if we would call upon Him (Jer. 33:3).

Jesus Prayed When He Was Tempted

Before He began His public ministry, Jesus spent
40 days fasting and praying in the wilderness (cf. Matt.
4:1-11; Lk. 4:1-13). During that time, He was tempted by
the devil. His steadfastness in prayer and ability to quote
Scripture ("the sword of the Spirit" – Eph. 6:17) gave Him

victory over temptation. He left the wilderness "in the power of the Spirit" (Lk. 4:14) and victorious.

Jesus was also tempted the night He was arrested in the Garden of Gethsemane. It was a special place of prayer for Jesus and His disciples where they often went (Jn. 18:2). There on the night before Jesus died, Satan tempted Him not to go to the cross. Jesus' prayer life helped Him resist that temptation. The writer of Hebrews describes Jesus' passionate prayers in Gethsemane by saying, "In the days of His flesh, He offered up both prayers and supplications with loud crying and tears to the One able to save Him from death, and He was heard because of His piety" (Heb. 5:7). The New International Version says, "He was heard because of His reverent submission." In earnest prayer, Jesus' surrendered to the Father's will that night, and overcame the temptation to turn away from the cross.

That same night Jesus also emphasized the power of prayer when He warned His disciples, "Keep watching and praying that you may not enter into temptation; the spirit is willing, but the flesh is weak" (Matt. 26:41). We will have victory over temptation only if we spend sufficient time in prayer.

Jesus Prayed While Suffering on the Cross

In the darkest six hours of His life, Jesus prayed. The Gospels record seven sayings that Jesus spoke while on the cross. Three of those sayings are prayers. "Father, forgive them; for they do not know what they are doing" (Lk. 23:34). The verb tense suggests that He prayed this prayer several times, perhaps for each person who had wronged Him during that previous night and day. Then, as C.H. Spurgeon said, it was "midnight at midday." Jesus prayed quoting from Psalm 22:1: "My God, My God, why have You forsaken Me?" (Matt. 27:46). The final words that Jesus uttered from the cross were also in the form of a prayer: "And Jesus, crying out with a loud voice, said, 'Father, into Your hands I commit My spirit.' Having said this, He breathed His last" (Lk. 23:46). Jesus' final words on the cross came verbatim from Psalm 31:5.

We can overcome the burdens, trials, and sufferings we encounter in this life just as our Savior did – through earnest prayer based on the powerful promises of the Word of God.

Jesus Prayed with Gratitude for God's Blessings

Jesus was thankful for the blessings God bestowed on Him while He was on earth. Jesus thanked the Father for listening to His prayers (Jn. 11:41-42). On another occasion, Jesus, "filled with the joy of the Holy Spirit," blessed and thanked the Father for giving special spiritual revelations to His followers who were childlike in their faith, unlike those who thought they were clever and wise (cf. Lk. 10:21).

One of the greatest examples of Jesus expressing gratitude to the Father in prayer took place after His resurrection. Jesus was in the town of Emmaus at the home of two of His disciples. The three of them had walked together some distance, but neither of His disciples had recognized Him. Their eyes were opened when He offered a prayer of thanksgiving and blessing for the meal just before He began to break the bread and distribute it to them (Lk. 24:30). The moment Jesus expressed thanks and broke the bread, they recognized Him. Isn't that amazing? Even in His resurrected state, our Lord would not put a morsel of food into His mouth before He thanked the Father for providing it. If we want to be like Jesus, we should follow His example of gratitude. We should, "Devote (ourselves) to prayer, keeping alert in it with an attitude of thanksgiving" (Col. 4:2).

Jesus Is Praying Right Now in Heaven!

The Bible tells us that when Jesus ascended to heaven, He entered triumphantly. While on earth, He was the sacrificial Lamb. In heaven, Jesus assumed the office of High Priest by applying His redemptive blood to the real Mercy Seat. It serves as an atoning sacrifice that has been paid for the sins of all mankind. He then sat down at the Father's right hand and began His mediatorial reign waiting for the day when God will make all His enemies a footstool for His feet (Ps. 110:1). He is now in heaven, seated on His glorious throne. And what is Jesus doing in His resurrected state? He is preparing heaven for His followers, pardoning lost people, and preparing to come again.

But Jesus is doing something else right now – praying for His people. "Therefore He is able also to save forever those who draw near to God through Him, since He always lives to make intercession for them" (Heb. 7:25). This verse links the security of our eternal salvation with the fact that Jesus will always pray on our behalf. Thus, if you are a Christian, you are going to make it safely through this life assured of the fact that you will enter into heaven when you die. All because Jesus is praying for you!

Jesus' Prayer Life – An Example for Us

The question we need to ask ourselves at this point is: "If Jesus, the divine, sinless, Spirit-filled Son of God needed to pray while He was on earth, don't we need to pray too?" Of course we do! If Jesus made prayer a priority, so should we!

Like Jesus, we should begin each day in an isolated place communing with the Father in prayer (cf. Mk. 1:35). I believe that is what Jesus had in mind when He said to His disciples, "But you, when you pray, go into your inner room, close your door and pray to your Father who is in secret, and your Father who sees what is done in secret will reward you" (Matt. 6:6). We "close (our) door" so we can enjoy a time of intimacy with the Father before we continue our day. Jesus is our example for this kind of praying!

Like Jesus, we should also take prayer retreats, perhaps even spending an entire night alone with God in prayer. We should pray before we make important decisions, when we are tempted, and when we suffer hardships. We should also pray regularly to express our gratitude for all of God's blessings, as well as pray for others just as Jesus prays for us.

Jesus' Prayer Life – an Encouragement to Us

One of the most encouraging things we can do for another person is to pray for him. We should not take the prayers of others for granted. The only thing more encouraging to me than hearing that someone is praying for me is the fact that Jesus Himself is praying for me. The Bible says, "Who is the one who condemns? Christ Jesus is He who died, yes, rather who was raised, who is at the right hand of God, who also intercedes for us" (Rom. 8:34). Jesus is for us, not against us, because He prays for us! What could be more encouraging than that?

Challenge:

How did Jesus accomplish so much in his short, 3½-year ministry? He rose every morning and communed with God in prayer. Prayer was a priority for Him. May it be a priority for us as well.

For Memory and Meditation:

"In the early morning, while it was still dark, Jesus got up, left the house, and went away to a secluded place, and was praying there" (Mark 1:35).

The Priority of Prayer: The Early Church

CHAPTER 2

Acts 1:14 – "These all with one mind were continually devoting themselves to prayer, along with the women, and Mary the mother of Jesus, and with His brothers."

The earliest Christians were prayer warriors. And where did they get their zeal for prayer? From Jesus Himself! Look at the Gospels and you will discover that the disciples asked Jesus to teach them only one thing. Not how to preach, how to grow a Sunday School, how to establish a seminary, how to conduct a choir or lead a praise band, how to properly administer the Lord's Supper, how to build a sanctuary, or how to collect financial offerings. They asked Jesus to teach them to pray. We read in Luke 11:1 – "It happened that while Jesus was praying in a certain place, after He had finished, one of His disciples said to Him, 'Lord, teach us to pray just as John also taught his disciples.'" They did not just ask Him to teach them *how* to pray, but to teach them *to* pray. Jesus' prayer life had impacted them so profoundly they wanted to learn to pray from the Master Himself.

As we read in Chapter 1, the Gospels show us that prayer was a priority for Jesus. When we read the Book of Acts, it is clear that Jesus' disciples also understood the significance of prayer.

The Early Church Began in a Ten-Day Prayer Meeting

At the opening of Acts, we see that the church was

9

a relatively small group of people. Their Master (Jesus) had left them and they were lacking the spiritual power they needed to carry out His command to evangelize the world. Just before He went back to heaven, Jesus had told them to wait in Jerusalem that they might be baptized with the Holy Spirit. The Spirit would endue them with the spiritual strength they needed to "make disciples of all the nations" (cf. Matt. 28:19-20). Jesus had said, "And now I will send the Holy Spirit, just as my Father promised. But stay here in the city until the Holy Spirit comes and fills you with power from heaven" (NLT Luke 24:49). He also told His disciples, "But you will receive power when the Holy Spirit comes upon you. And you will be my witnesses, telling people about me everywhere – in Jerusalem, throughout Judea, in Samaria, and to the ends of the earth" (NLT Acts 1:8).

The time between Jesus' resurrection and ascension was forty days (cf. Acts 1:3). After he went back to heaven, approximately ten days passed before the Spirit came upon the believers. That small band of Christ followers gathered in an upper room in Jerusalem fellowshipping, taking care of church business, and, above all, praying. "They all met together and were constantly united in prayer, along with Mary the mother of Jesus, several other women, and the brothers of Jesus" (NLT Acts 1:14).

When the day of Pentecost arrived, the Spirit came upon the members of that prayer meeting and infused them with heavenly power. They left the upper room and went out among the people gathered in Jerusalem. As they met the many Jewish people who had traveled there from all over the Roman Empire, each of those

Spirit-filled believers began miraculously "speaking of the mighty deeds of God" in the languages of the people who were listening to them (Acts 2:11). Soon afterward, Peter preached and three thousand people were saved!

How could something like that happen? They prayed passionately for ten days, the Holy Spirit filled them with power, the people shared, Peter preached the Gospel and gave an invitation, and people responded by repenting of sin, putting their faith in Jesus, and calling on His name to save them. And it all started with prayer. The early church was literally birthed in a prayer meeting! If we want to be like those early believers, we must pray.

God "Shakes" Us through Prayer

When Peter and John were on their way to the Temple in Jerusalem "at the hour of prayer" (cf. Acts 3:1), they met a lame beggar lying at the Beautiful Gate. When he requested a gift from the Apostles, Peter told him they had no money, but they had something better! He told the man, "In the name of Jesus, rise up and walk!" He then took the man by the hand and helped him to his feet. The man began to walk, leap, and praise God as he entered the Temple with the apostles. A crowd gathered, Peter preached, and many believed in Jesus.

These events infuriated the Jewish religious leaders. They arrested Peter and John and commanded them to stop speaking in the name of Jesus. The disciples refused, insisting that they "could not stop speaking of what (they had) seen and heard" (Acts 4:20). When they were released, the disciples went back to the other Christians and engaged in an intense time of prayer. They asked the

Lord to grant them boldness to declare the Gospel and to extend His powerful hand so that many would be healed, and that signs and wonders would continue to take place in the powerful name of Jesus (cf. Acts 4:29-30). In the middle of their prayer time, God did something unusual. Acts 4:31 says, "And when they had prayed, the place where they had gathered together was shaken, and they were all filled with the Holy Spirit and began to speak the word of God with boldness." God shook them physically and spiritually.

I believe that our churches today could use a good spiritual "shaking." The early Christians prayed, God shook them by filling them with His Spirit, and then He shook the world as they witnessed boldly for Christ. God ministered through them to perform mighty miracles. There was no way they were going to keep silent. They had "seen and heard" too much from their Lord. Their lives had been radically changed. It all began with prayer!

Perhaps if we would pray as they did, we too would be "shaken." We just might "see and hear" more from the Lord than we do presently.

Prayer Should Precede Preaching and Witnessing

When I was in college, I took voice lessons to learn how to sing. My instructor's first lesson was this: "Before you can sing well, you must learn how to breathe correctly." He was referring to the art of breathing and singing diaphragmatically. Just as a singer must learn to breathe properly before he can sing, a Christian must learn to pray before he can proclaim the Gospel with power.

The Church in Jerusalem grew quickly in its earliest

days. In the midst of that growth, a dispute broke out among the widows regarding the distribution of food. When the problem was brought to the apostles for them to solve, they refused to get involved. Instead, they instructed the church to select seven men (I believe they were the first deacons). Those men were to be filled with the Holy Spirit and wisdom. They could deal with issues such as the dispute among the senior adults over food. Meanwhile, the apostles told the church, "But we will devote ourselves to prayer and to the ministry of the word" (Acts 6:4).

Notice that they mentioned "prayer" prior to "preaching." A coincidence? I think not. We read something similar in Mark 3:13-15: "And He (Jesus) went up on the mountain and summoned those whom He Himself wanted, and they came to Him. And He appointed twelve, so that they would be with Him and that He could send them out to preach, and to have authority to cast out the demons." We see the same priority in these verses. Jesus appointed the disciples to: 1) "be with Him," 2) "preach," and 3) "cast out demons" – in that order! Before they went out to preach, they would spend time with Jesus. Before they commanded demons to leave people, they would spend time conversing with the Savior.

Like the early believers, we have no business trying to talk *for* God in preaching and witnessing until we have first talked *with* God in prayer. Passionate prayer precedes persuasive preaching and successful soul winning. Prayerless preaching and prayerless witnessing bear little fruit (if any). We must learn to talk with God before we try to talk about God to others. It all begins with prayer.

God Speaks to Us When We Pray

One day, as Peter prayed on a rooftop at noon at a home in the city of Joppa (Acts 10:9), he had a vision. God told him, "What God has cleansed, no longer consider unholy" (Acts 10:15). The Lord was speaking to Peter about a sin in his life – prejudice. God told him not to be prejudiced toward Gentiles.

At the same time, God was preparing the heart of a Gentile named Cornelius just north of Joppa in the city of Caesarea. Cornelius had also been praying. An angel told him that God had heard his prayers and that a man named Peter was coming to share the Gospel of Christ with him. When Peter came to Cornelius' home, he entered without reservation even though it was socially forbidden for Jews to enter the home of a Gentile. He shared the Gospel with Cornelius, and he and his entire family were saved.

Unfortunately, our world is filled with prejudice today. People hate other people who have different colored skin. But God used prayer to tear down the wall of prejudice and racism in Peter's life, and He can do the same for us as well.

God Works Miracles When We Pray

King Herod Agrippa arrested the apostles, James and Peter. His soldiers killed James with a sword. Peter was imprisoned, awaiting trial and likely death. But the church prayed fervently for Peter (Acts 12:5). That night while Peter was asleep between two soldiers, an angel appeared in his cell. Peter's chains fell off and the angel led him out of the prison unharmed. He then went to the church where many believers were still gathered in prayer on his behalf. When they saw Peter, they realized that God had done a mighty work.

Has God lost His power? Would He not do more mighty deeds like this in our day if we "prayed the price?" I believe God is waiting for us to pray before He will unleash His limitless, miracle-working power. Where prayer focuses, God's power falls! It all begins with prayer.

God Calls People to Missions When We Pray

A group of prophets and teachers gathered at the Church of Antioch to minister to the Lord through prayer, worship, and fasting. There the Holy Spirit set apart the first "missionaries" (cf. Acts 13:1f). After they prayed and fasted again, the group laid hands on Paul and Barnabas and sent them out. Those men planted churches that reproduced other churches throughout the Roman Empire, and the world has never been the same.

What would have happened if that little group in Antioch had been sitting around talking about mundane things rather than seeking first the kingdom of God? If we would host more prayer meetings in our churches and fewer committee meetings, God would call more people and the Gospel would spread throughout the world at a swifter pace. Again, it all begins with prayer.

Challenge:

The Book of Acts goes on to tell of many more victories wrought by prayer. The fact is – God works through praying people. Your theology may be correct, but if your prayer life is anemic, your work is in vain. As my friend,

Don Miller says, "What good is a prayerless conservative?"

God moves when we pray! There are some things God does whether we pray or not. But there are other things God will do only when we pray. Prayer really does "change things." It was a priority for the earliest Christians. Prayer accessed the power they needed to turn their world upside down. May we seek God in prayer as they did. When we do, I believe we will see similar results. It all begins with prayer!

For Memory and Meditation:

"These all with one mind were continually devoting themselves to prayer, along with the women, and Mary the mother of Jesus, and with His brothers" (Acts 1:14).

The Lord's Prayer - A Pattern for Prayer – (Part 1)

CHAPTER 3

When Jesus' disciples asked Him to teach them to pray, He answered by giving them (and us) a model prayer commonly referred to as "The Lord's Prayer" (Lk. 11:1f). In His famous Sermon on the Mount, Jesus expanded that great prayer. In this chapter, we will analyze the initial words He gave to His disciples.

Pray, then, in this way: "Our Father who is in heaven, Hallowed be Your name. Your kingdom come. Your will be done, on earth as it is in heaven. Give us this day our daily bread" (Matt. 6:9-11).

Jesus didn't want this prayer to be memorized and prayed by rote. Instead, He intended it to be a model prayer for His followers to use as one of the greatest patterns for prayer in all of Scripture.

Our Father Who Is in Heaven

The Lord's Prayer begins with, "Our Father who is in heaven." Jesus emphasized our need to praise God as our "Father." The "front door" that a Christian enters to engage in prayer is the door of praise. The Psalmist concurred when he said, "Enter His gates with thanksgiving and His courts with praise. Give thanks to Him, bless His name" (NAU Psalm 100:4).

God is the Creator of all people. But God is the Father only to those who know Him in salvation through His Son, Jesus Christ. The Apostle Paul reminded the Galatian Christians of this when he said, "Because you are sons,

God has sent forth the Spirit of His Son into our hearts, crying, 'Abba! Father!'" (^NAU Gal. 4:6).

Before you can pray, you must be assured that you really are a Christian and that God is indeed your "Father." Scripture says, "Test yourselves to see if you are in the faith; examine yourselves! Or do you not recognize this about yourselves, that Jesus Christ is in you – unless indeed you fail the test?" (^NAU 2 Cor. 13:5). Do not merely ask yourself if you are a church member, because church membership does not guarantee salvation. Rather, examine yourself and ask yourself if you have really been saved.

When was it that as a non-Christian you volitionally recognized and acknowledged that you are a sinner by nature (Eph. 2:1-3) and by choice (Isa. 53:6)? When did you repent and turn from your sins (Acts 3:19) placing all of your faith and trust completely in Jesus for salvation (Acts 16:30-31; Rom. 5:1)? When did you confess with your mouth that Jesus is your Lord and believe in your heart that Jesus died for your sins, and that God raised Him from the dead? At what point in time did you call upon the name of the Lord Jesus and ask Him to save you (Rom. 10:9-13)? When did you receive and accept Jesus as your personal Lord and Savior (John 1:12), experiencing "the washing of regeneration and renewing of the Holy Spirit" (Titus 3:5)? When were you "born again" (Jn. 3:7)? You might not remember the exact date, but you certainly should remember something substantive about such a life-altering experience.

No one has "always been saved." Regeneration is an instantaneous, punctiliar experience. It takes place at a specific nanosecond in time. Before regeneration, you were lost and on your way to hell. After regeneration, you are saved and on your way to heaven. Regeneration is pictured in the New Testament as God's gracious response to man's repentance from sin and believing in His Son, Jesus. In the New Testament, regeneration always follows repentance and faith; it never precedes it. Scripture unilaterally declares that when someone repents and believes, regeneration occurs. As one famous Greek scholar says regarding salvation, "'Grace' is God's part, 'faith' ours."[1] We are saved when we repent of sin, believe in Jesus, and receive Him as Lord and Savior calling on His name – plain and simple.

This is significant because it is not until we know for certain (cf. Jn. 5:24; 1 Jn. 5:13) that we have been genuinely converted to Christ that we will be able to genuinely pray to God as "Our Father who is in heaven!" Only with such assurance can any believer in Jesus pray to God and worship Him intimately according to the names ascribed to Him in Scripture.

Hallowed Be Your Name

Once you are certain that you are saved, then you are ready to pray, "Hallowed be Your name." Throughout the Bible, the one, true God is referred to by various names. Each name reveals an aspect of His divine nature and character. Here are some of the names of God that prove helpful to a believer as he worships and praises God as his "Father." In the Old Testament, God was referred to with names such as…

[1.] A.T. Robertson, *Word Pictures in the New Testament,* *Vol. 4,* (Nashville: Broadman Press, 1931), p. 525

- Jehovah-Jireh – The Lord My Provider (Genesis 22:14).

- Jehovah-Rapha – The Lord Who Heals (Exodus 15:26).

- Jehovah-Nissi – The Lord My Banner (Exodus 17:15-16).

- Jehovah-Makadesh – The Lord Who Sanctifies (Leviticus 20:7-8).

- Jehovah-Shalom – The Lord My Peace (Judges 6:24).

- Jehovah-Rohi – The Lord My Shepherd (Psalm 23:1).

- Jehovah-Tsidkenu – The Lord My Righteousness (Jeremiah 23:5-6).

- Jehovah-Shammah – The Lord Who Is Present (Ezekiel 48:35).

Similarly, there are various names ascribed to Jesus in the New Testament that are also helpful in our prayer time as we worship God. Some of those names point to the fact that Jesus is…

- The Bread of Life (John 6:35).

- The Light of the World (John 8:12).

- The Door of the Sheep (John 10:7).

- The Good Shepherd (John 10:11, 14).

- The Resurrection and the Life (John 11:25).

- The Way, the Truth, and the Life (John 14:6).

- The True Vine (John 15:1).

So how does this work? How can we utilize these names attributed to God in our prayers? Allow me to illustrate.

Using God's Name to Pray

We can praise and thank God for His provision and blessings by praying, "Father, I bless You today that You are Jehovah-Jireh, the Lord My Provider! Thank You that You will supply all of my needs according to Your riches in glory in Christ Jesus (Phil. 4:19). Praise You that "You who did not spare Your own Son, but delivered Him up for us all, how will you not also with Jesus freely give to me all things that I need (Rom. 8:32)?"

Similarly, we can thank God for His protection by praying, "Father, I praise You that You are Jehovah-Nissi, the Lord my Banner. Thank You that You fight for me while I keep silent (Ex. 14:14). Your word declares that "the battle is the Lord's" (1 Sam. 17:47). Thank You that today no evil will befall me, nor will any plague come near my dwelling. You will give your angels charge concerning me to guard me in all of my ways (Ps. 91:10-11). You will strengthen and protect me from the evil one (2 Thess. 3:3). I acknowledge my complete dependence on Your protection. "Unless You guard me and my family, every other watchman keeps awake in vain (Ps. 127:1)."

To be sure, we must never disassociate any Scripture from its context. But the Bible comes alive when we faithfully interpret verses and apply them as promises regarding our needs and situations. God is still God. He wants to show Himself mighty in our day. His names indicate who He is and how He desires to move today. If Scripture states that God provided for or protected someone in the past, today's believer has every reason to ask God to do the same for him. God is still alive and so is His Word!

Your Kingdom Come. Your Will Be Done

Once the believer has worshiped and thanked God that He is his "Father" because of Jesus, and has worshiped Him according to the various names ascribed to Him in Scripture, then he can surrender himself as a living sacrifice to the Lord and request that God's perfect will be accomplished in his life. That is what Jesus taught in the words, "Your kingdom come. Your will be done, on earth as it is in heaven" (Matt. 6:10).

Jesus wants each of His children to surrender daily to His will. This attitude characterized Jesus' mother as well as Jesus Himself. Before Jesus was conceived, the angel Gabriel visited Jesus' future mother, Mary, who lived in Nazareth. Gabriel informed her that God had chosen her to bear the Messiah. She questioned how that could be possible since she was a virgin. Dr. Herschel Hobbs used to say, "The first one to question the virginal birth of Jesus was the virgin herself!" Gabriel explained that the Holy Spirit would come upon Mary and she would miraculously conceive Jesus, the Messiah. Mary's humble, submissive response was, "Behold, the bondslave of the Lord; may it be done to me according to your word" ([NAU] Lk. 1:38). Mary surrendered completely to God's will.

Jesus did the same when He struggled in prayer in the Garden of Gethsemane the night before He was crucified. Jesus was not a coward and did not fear physical death. Instead, His righteous, sinless soul recoiled from the idea of drinking the bitter cup of God's wrath by dying on the cross as an atoning sacrifice bearing the sins of all mankind. In obedience to God, He who knew no sin would become sin on our behalf so that we might become the righteousness of God (cf. 2 Cor. 5:21). That is what Jesus submissively embraced in Gethsemane. He offered Himself to the Father's will with the infamous words, "Your will be done" (Matt. 26:39, 42). While salvation was realized at Calvary, Jesus' surrendered will paved the way for salvation the night before in Gethsemane!

Are you surrendered to the will of God? Before we know God's will, we must surrender ourselves to it. Are you willing to die to your selfish desires (Lk. 9:23) and ask God to accomplish His perfect will in every area of your life?

Give Us This Day Our Daily Bread

God is a good Father to His children. Based on that relationship with Him, He instructs us to ask Him to meet our needs (Matt. 7:11). Someone has wisely said, "God will meet all of our *need*, but NOT all of our *greed*." We must learn to be content with what He grants us (1 Tim. 6:8). The same God who gave us His Son, Jesus Christ, will also give us everything we need in life to do His will (Rom.

8:32). Each morning we are to ask God to supply us with whatever we need to serve Him that day. He will answer and do so abundantly (Eph. 3:20-21).

Challenge:

Do you know God in salvation? Is God really your "Father"? If not, repent of your sin and place your faith and trust in Jesus alone for your salvation. Call upon Jesus' name and receive Him as your Lord and Savior. Once you have nailed that personal relationship down, begin to praise God as your heavenly "Father," enjoying the intimacy that is rightfully yours through the covenant God has made with you through Christ in salvation.

Then, using the names ascribed to God throughout the Bible, worship and adore the Lord. Use the samples in this chapter and look for other names mentioned throughout Scripture that describe the amazing nature and character of the one true God. Learn to "Give thanks to Him and bless His name" (Ps. 100:4b)!

Next, surrender yourself completely to God's will. Offer yourself as a living and holy sacrifice to Him (Rom. 12:1-2), learn to die daily (1 Cor. 15:31; Gal. 2:20) to your selfishness, yielding to His will.

As you follow Jesus' words, you will see that the Lord's Prayer is indeed a helpful pattern for communing with your heavenly Father!

For Memory and Meditation:

"And those who know Your name will put their trust in You, for You, O LORD, have not forsaken those who seek You" (NAU Psalm 9:10).

The Lord's Prayer - A Pattern for Prayer — (Part 2)

CHAPTER 4

As we saw in Chapter 3, when Jesus' disciples asked Him to teach them to pray, He answered by giving them (and us) a model prayer commonly referred to as "The Lord's Prayer" (Lk. 11:1f). In this chapter, we will analyze the concluding words that Jesus gave to His disciples.

"Pray, then, in this way: . . . 'And forgive us our debts, as we also have forgiven our debtors. 'And do not lead us into temptation, but deliver us from evil. For Yours is the kingdom and the power and the glory forever. Amen'" (^{NAU} Matt. 6:9, 12-13).

Forgive Us as We Forgive Others

The next step in the Lord's pattern for prayer deals with forgiveness. As Christians, we need to ask the Father to forgive our sins. A person becomes a Christian by repenting of sin, believing in Jesus, and calling on Jesus' name for salvation. When a person does this from a sincere heart, the Holy Spirit regenerates him, and he is "born again" (Jn. 3:7). When a person becomes a Christian, he does not enter into a state of sinless perfection. Rather, he continues to commit sins. The Bible says: "If we say that we have no sin, we are deceiving ourselves and the truth is not in us" (^{NAU} 1 Jn. 1:8), and, "If we say that we have not sinned, we make Him a liar and His word is not in us" (^{NAU} 1 Jn. 1:10).

John also tells Christians what to do when they sin. The words he spoke between the two verses just mentioned are some of the most comforting Scriptures in the Bible. "If we confess our sins, He is faithful and righteous to forgive us our sins and to cleanse us from all unrighteousness" ([NAU] 1 Jn. 1:9). To "confess" means "to agree with and say the same thing" about our sins that God does. We admit that we have transgressed His laws and have behaved rebelliously. As believers our sins do not cause us to lose our relationship with God, but they do impede our fellowship with God. When we confess our sins to Him, He graciously forgives us and restores that fellowship.

Jesus follows this by saying that we must also forgive other people who have sinned against us. We must ask God to forgive us in the same way that we forgive those who wrong us. It is noteworthy that this section of the Lord's Prayer is the only place where Jesus makes a comment to expand what He has just said – "For if you forgive others for their transgressions, your heavenly Father will also forgive you. [15] But if you do not forgive others, then your Father will not forgive your transgressions" ([NAU] Matt. 6:14-15).

When we harbor bitterness and unforgiveness in our hearts toward those who have wronged us, we put ourselves in a dangerous position with God. Unforgiveness is a sign of our pride and ingratitude. We are setting ourselves up as a judge of others. God alone is capable of rightly judging (Jam. 4:12). We also display ingratitude that God has forgiven our sins (Matt. 18:21-35). If we want forgiveness, we must forgive others, whether they ask for forgiveness or not. That's exactly what Jesus did when He was crucified (Lk. 23:34). That does not mean that we condone what someone did to us, nor does it mean that we must trust them in the future. But we do have to "pardon" him if we want to be pardoned by God (Lk. 6:37).

Do Not Lead Us into Temptation

Next, Jesus teaches us to pray some "preventive prayers." We are to pray, "And do not lead us into temptation." God does not tempt anyone to sin, nor does He predestine anyone to sin. God does not predestine what He prohibits in Scripture. God cannot be against God.

James assures us of this when he writes, "Let no one say when he is tempted, 'I am being tempted by God'; for God cannot be tempted by evil, and He Himself does not tempt anyone" (NAU Jam. 1:13). God is absolutely pure, holy, sinless "light," in Whom there is no sin whatsoever (1 Jn. 1:5). Our sin comes from our sinful nature, which we inherited from Adam (Rom. 5:12; Jam. 1:14). We should ask God to lead us away from sin into righteousness, for it is God's desire to lead us "in paths of righteousness for His name's sake" (Ps. 23:3).

At the beginning of each day we should pray about everything on our schedule and ask God to help us to be holy and Christlike in every situation. This puts us in the right frame of mind to be on guard against the temptations of Satan. When we ask God to help us battle temptation, He listens and answers our prayers!

Remember that being tempted is the norm for everyone, even Christians. Our adversary, the devil, never stops tempting us to sin. He even tempted Jesus (cf. Lk. 4:13), but Jesus refused to yield to his temptation. Rather, Jesus overcame temptation by fasting, praying, and quoting Scripture.

God says, "No temptation has overtaken you but such as is common to man; and God is faithful, who will not allow you to be tempted beyond what you are able, but with the temptation will provide the way of escape also, so that you will be able to endure it" (^NAU 1 Cor. 10:13). Whenever we are tempted, we should ask God to show us "the way of escape." Sometimes it will mean that we should "flee" from temptation. For example, we are told to flee from "immorality" (1 Cor. 6:18), "idolatry" (1 Cor. 10:14), "the love of money" (1 Tim. 6:10-11), and "youthful lusts" (2 Tim. 2:22). God wants us to win the battle against sin by avoiding temptation. As Barney Fife would say, "Nip it in the bud!"

Deliver Us from Evil

At other times we are told to "submit to God and resist the devil" (Jam. 4:7), and "stand firm against the schemes of the devil" (Eph. 6:11). That's why Jesus went on to say in the Lord's Prayer, "but deliver us from evil." The word "evil" is accompanied by the definite article "the" because Jesus was actually referring to "the evil one" (i.e. Satan). The same devil that tempted Jesus to sin tempts us as well.

Some Christians try to downplay the fact that Satan opposes and oppresses Christians. The early Christians certainly did not agree with such thinking. Paul warned believers by saying, "Do not give the devil a foothold" (^NIV Eph. 4:27). He also said, "Our struggle is not against flesh and blood, but against the rulers, against the powers, against the world forces of this darkness, against the spiritual forces of wickedness in the heavenly places" (^NAU Eph. 6:12). Paul later pointed out that during his walk with

Jesus "a messenger of Satan buffeted" him (2 Cor. 12:7), and that Satan himself had even "thwarted" him (1 Thess. 2:18). Paul was "not ignorant of (Satan's) schemes" (2 Cor. 2:11). Likewise, both James and Peter warn us to "resist the devil" (cf. Jam. 4:7; 1 Pet. 5:8-9).

Jesus said to His disciples in ^{NAU} Lk. 10:19 – "Behold, I have given you authority to tread on serpents and scorpions, and over all the power of the enemy, and nothing will injure you." These "serpents and scorpions" refer to demonic "evil spirits" (cf. Lk. 10:20). God has given every believer in Christ this same authority and power over the forces of Satan. The devil is not afraid of Christians, but he is afraid of Christ in us (1 Jn. 4:4)!

God gives us authority over Satan through the name of Jesus, the blood of Jesus, and the Word of God. Paul cast an evil spirit out of a demonized fortuneteller "in the name of Jesus Christ" (Acts 16:18). He also told us to stand against the devil's attacks using the sword of the Spirit, the Word of God (Eph. 6:17). That is why each time Satan tempted Jesus, our Lord quoted Scripture against him (cf. Matt. 4:1f & Lk. 4:1f). We also have the power of the covering of the blood of Jesus to help us overcome the attacks of the devil (Rev. 12:11). With all these weapons, there is no reason to allow Satan to frighten or discourage us.

Sadly, there are many Christians who have been forgiven of their sins and are on their way to heaven, yet they are living with sinful strongholds. God has equipped us with powerful spiritual weapons to tear down such strongholds (cf. 2 Cor. 10:3-5). A stronghold of sin in the life of a believer is simply "a house of lies" that he believes instead of trusting in the truth of God's Word. If we abide in Jesus and His Word abides in us, we will know the truth and it will set us free (Jn. 8:31-32). All Christians are forgiven, but not all Christians are walking in victory and freedom.

The Christian life is a battleground, not a playground. A Christian is a "soldier of Jesus Christ" (2 Tim. 2:3). We are in a war and we must fight the good fight against Satan in order to experience daily victory!

The Kingdom and the Power and the Glory Forever

Finally, Jesus taught us to close our prayer time the way we began it – by praising God. He concludes by saying, "For Yours is the kingdom and the power and the glory forever." These words are similar to those in Revelation when God was worshiped and praised in heaven (cf. Rev. 4:11; 5:12).

According to these verses, God is to be praised as the King of all kings and Lord of all lords who reigns sovereignly over everything that exists. As one preacher said, "You cannot impeach God, and He is not going to resign!" God is also to be exalted and worshiped because He is omnipotent. Nothing is too difficult for Him (Jer. 32:17). Finally, He is to be exalted and praised because He is glorious. He is worshiped perpetually in heaven as the glorious and holy God. His glory extends throughout the Universe. And then at the end of our prayers, we are to say, "Amen!" When we say that, we are saying, "So be it, Lord!" It is in this manner that we are to pray!

Challenge:

If we want to pray as Jesus wants us to, we must ask

God to forgive us when we commit sins. If you currently have unconfessed sin in your life, repent of it, confess it, and forsake it immediately.

After you are cleansed and forgiven, it is time to forgive anyone who has wronged you. Pardon them and release them from the cage of bitterness and unforgiveness in which you have selfishly and pridefully imprisoned them. When you forgive them, God will forgive you.

Then engage in spiritual warfare. Put on the whole armor of God, stand on the truth of God's Word and stand strong in the power of Jesus' shed blood. Submit to God and resist the devil in the authority of Jesus' omnipotent name.

As you end your time of prayer, praise God as your King who is all-powerful and glorious. Conclude by praying "In Jesus' name (Jn. 16:24), Amen!" as you ask God to do exceedingly, abundantly beyond all that you could ever ask or think!

For Memory and Meditation:

"Therefore, confess your sins to one another, and pray for one another so that you may be healed. The effective prayer of a righteous man can accomplish much" (NAU Jam. 5:16).

What Hinders Our Prayers?

CHAPTER 5

Most Bible-believing Christians acknowledge that prayer is critically important to experiencing a vibrant walk with Christ. Yet those same people would also admit that from time to time certain things hinder them from spending time in prayer with the Lord. What are these hindrances and how can we overcome them?

Busyness

Someone has said, "If the devil cannot make you bad, he will try to make you busy." Busyness is one of the great enemies of effective prayer. Perhaps the classic example in Scripture is the contrast between two sisters, Mary and Martha, who lived during Jesus' day in the small town of Bethany outside of Jerusalem. When Jesus came to see them, Martha became busy preparing a meal for Jesus, while her sister, Mary, took time to sit at Jesus' feet and listen to His word. In the end, Jesus commended Mary and rebuked Martha. He told them both that time spent alone with Him in meditation and prayer was more important than anything else (Lk. 10:38-42).

If you are too busy to pray, then you are too busy. You must "seek first His kingdom" (Matt. 6:33) by spending time with God in prayer. If you do not make time for talking with God, God might "readjust" your schedule for you until you have plenty of time to talk with Him.

Disobedience

When a Christian disobeys the Lord, approaching Him in prayer becomes difficult. To be sure, we are saved by grace, not works. Nevertheless, Scripture consistently teaches that God blesses obedience and punishes disobedience. John the Apostle reminds us that God blesses our obedience by answering our prayers. John said, "And whatever we ask we receive from Him, because we keep His commandments and do the things that are pleasing in His sight" (NAU 1 Jn. 3:22). There is a direct connection between, "ask and receive" and "keep His commandments and do the things that are pleasing in His sight."

Obedience is a choice, and so is disobedience. We can choose to do the right thing and blessings will follow. When we choose to spend time with God reading His Word, He blesses us by speaking to us and guiding us. When we choose to tithe and give offerings to our church, He blesses and takes care of our needs. When we choose to join with other Christians in corporate worship, He blesses us with spiritually stimulating encouragement. But when we disobey Him, He disciplines us, and prayer becomes increasingly difficult.

Laziness

Sometimes we fail to pray because we are undisciplined and slothful. We use our time poorly, failing to understand that to "waste time" is to "waste life." Of course, God knows we cannot work 24 hours a day, seven days a week. That's why He introduced the concept of the Sabbath. Yet God does want us to use our time wisely and spend significant portions of that time with Him in prayer.

Peter said, "Be earnest and disciplined in your prayers" (^{NLT} 1 Pet. 4:7b). Lethargic prayers do not move the heart and hand of God (Jam. 4:2). That is why Paul encourages us to "Discipline (ourselves) for the purpose of godliness" (^{NAU} 1 Tim. 4:7). And that certainly includes spending time in prayer.

Idolatry

The first two of the Ten Commandments say, "You shall have no other gods before Me. You shall not make for yourself an idol" (^{NAU} Ex. 20:3-4a). When we hear or read the word, "idol," we might immediately think of a stone statue of a pagan deity before which someone bows reverently and burns incense. But the concept of idolatry is more complex than that. Idolatry has many expressions. We are guilty of idolatry anytime something or someone becomes more significant to us and more influential in our life than God Himself.

For instance, the love of money is certainly an idol. An overemphasis on and love for material possessions can also be indicative of idolatry. Nowadays, athletics and sports often become idolatrous. Some people are so engrossed in sports they refuse to go to church on Sunday when their favorite college football team loses a game on Saturday!

Idolatry is viewed in Scripture as spiritual adultery against God. It is bestowing love and reverence to an undeserving object in an inappropriate manner. The Old Testament prophets warned God's people about the dangers of idolatry, as did the apostles in the New Testament. The Apostle John concluded his first letter by saying, "Little children, guard yourselves from idols" ([NAU] 1 Jn. 5:21). When you love someone or something more than Jesus, it makes talking with God difficult.

Unforgiveness

In Chapter 4, we learned that when we fail to forgive others, God refuses to forgive us. When we harbor bitterness and unforgiveness, the Lord turns a deaf ear to our prayers. Jesus commented on His famous "Lord's Prayer" with these sobering words, "For if you forgive others for their transgressions, your heavenly Father will also forgive you. But if you do not forgive others, then your Father will not forgive your transgressions" ([NAU] Matt. 6:14-15).

Years ago I knew a Christian man who was a stellar believer in Jesus. He loved the Lord, his family, his church, and he was a soul winner. But when his parents died, he and his siblings began to argue over their parents' estate. Before long, they had engaged in a bitter dispute that severed their fellowship with one another. That man tarnished his witness simply because he and his brothers and sisters became greedy and acted hatefully toward one another, allowing themselves to become bitter and unforgiving.

Someone has said, "Bitterness is an acid that destroys its own container." When we are bitter and refuse to forgive those who have wronged us, it short-circuits our prayers. Jesus forgave those who crucified Him even though they did not ask for forgiveness (cf. Lk. 23:34). Deacon Stephen died while forgiving those who were executing him (Acts 7:60). When you refuse to forgive other people who have wronged you, God refuses to forgive you.

Unconfessed Sin

The Lord said in Psalms that if we harbor sin in our lives, He will not even hear our prayers, much less answer them. We read in ^{NAU} Ps. 66:18 – "If I regard wickedness in my heart, the Lord will not hear." If a Christian harbors unconfessed sin in his life, it stifles the effectiveness of his prayers.

Every Christian sins after he becomes a believer in Jesus. When a Christian sins, he does not lose his salvation, but he does lose the joy of his salvation (Ps. 51:12). Like filth clogs a drain or an obstruction severs an electrical circuit, sin kills prayer. For the anointing of the Holy Spirit to begin flowing again in our lives, we must confess and repent of our sins. "He who conceals his transgressions will not prosper, but he who confesses and forsakes them will find compassion" (^{NAU} Prov. 28:13).

Get alone with the Lord and pray: "Father, please reveal to me any and all sin in my life of which I have not repented." Pray Ps. 139:23-24, which says, "Search me, O God, and know my heart; try me and know my anxious thoughts; and see if there be any hurtful way in me, and lead me in the everlasting way." If there is any unconfessed sin in your life, the Holy Spirit will gently and specifically reveal it. Confess it as sin, repent of it, and ask God to forgive you. Then claim His forgiveness by faith. Afterwards, ask the Lord to fill you afresh with His Holy Spirit (Lk. 11:13). If you want to talk with God in prayer, get rid of your sin!

Family Strife

You cannot be right with God when you have wrong relationships within your immediate family. God says that children who are at home and still under their parents' authority are to "honor and obey" their parents (Eph. 6:1-3). Likewise, when your relationship with your spouse is not right, your prayers will be hindered. The Apostle Peter says, "You husbands in the same way, live with your wives in an understanding way, as with someone weaker, since she is a woman; and show her honor as a fellow heir of the grace of life, so that your prayers will not be hindered" (NAU 1 Pet. 3:7). Marriage is God's picture of how the church ought to relate to Jesus. Jesus is our husband; we are His wife (Eph. 5:22-27). Husbands are to lovingly lead their families just as Christ loves and leads the church. Wives are to respectively submit to their husbands just as the church does to Christ.

The modern movement to "redefine" marriage from being exclusively between one man and one woman for life is satanic. Jesus' teachings categorically affirm heterosexual marriage while also prohibiting divorce, except for adultery. God takes family seriously, and so should believers in Jesus.

Lack of Faith

God does not just want us to pray. He wants us to pray in faith. Jesus often said something to this effect: "Then He touched their eyes, saying, 'It shall be done to you according to your faith'" (NAU Matt. 9:29). James, the half-brother of Jesus, also said, "But if any of you lacks wisdom, let him ask of God, who gives to all generously and without reproach, and it will be given to him. But he must ask in faith without any doubting, for the one who doubts is like the surf of the sea, driven and tossed by the wind. For that man ought not to expect that he will receive anything from the Lord, being a double-minded man, unstable in all his ways" (^{NAU} Jam. 1:5-8). Prayer and faith go together, just as doubting and unanswered prayer go together. Some people recoil when they hear the phrase, "Prayer changes things." They believe that God has already predestined everything that is going to happen, therefore, prayer does not really change anything. It simply acknowledges a Christian's willingness to accept whatever the Lord has decreed.

Yet there are many instances mentioned throughout the Bible that clearly teach that God moved in a certain situation in a specific manner simply because someone prayed in faith and believed that God would act. One tremendous example is when God healed Hezekiah because he prayed. God said in 2 Kings. 20:5, "I have heard your prayer, I have seen your tears; behold, I will heal you." God did not say, "I have already decided to heal you, but go ahead and pray in agreement with my foreordained decision." No indeed! God heard Hezekiah's faith-filled prayer and then gave a miraculous answer to that great intercessor! Others like Elijah also prayed in faith, and the windows of heaven were shut. He prayed again, and then they were opened (cf. James 5:17-18).

God must be the sole object of our faith when we pray. We are to believe in Him (Jn. 14:1). Without faith, we cannot possibly please Him (Heb. 11:6). Anything that we do that is not of faith is sin (Rom. 14:23). Christians are to walk by faith, not by sight (2 Cor. 5:7). We are saved through faith (Eph. 2:8) and we are to pray in faith (Mk. 11:22-24). Faith is the missing ingredient. When we pray in faith, God acts!

Challenge:

What is hindering your prayer life? Whatever it might be, it is not worth having your requests discarded by God. Anything that hinders your prayer life is against God's will. Rid yourself of it immediately. Check first in some of these common areas just mentioned: busyness, disobedience, laziness, idolatry, unforgiveness, unconfessed sin, family strife, and lack of faith. When you discover what it is that hinders your prayers, take radical measures to rid yourself of it.

For Memory and Meditation:

"If I regard wickedness in my heart, the Lord will not hear" (NAU Ps. 66:18).

What Helps Our Prayers?

CHAPTER 6

Even as there are hindrances to prayer, there are also principles that will help us pray to the Father as we should. What are these helps to prayer and how can we as believers in Jesus benefit from them?

The Holy Spirit

The Holy Spirit is referred to in Scripture as the believer's Helper. Jesus said, "I will ask the Father, and He will give you another Helper, that He may be with you forever; that is the Spirit of truth, whom the world cannot receive, because it does not see Him or know Him, but you know Him because He abides with you and will be in you" (NAU Jn. 14:16). The Holy Spirit, who lives within every believer, will help every believer in every aspect of the Christian life, including the area of prayer.

Paul said, "In the same way the Spirit also helps our weakness; for we do not know how to pray as we should, but the Spirit Himself intercedes for us with groanings too deep for words; and He who searches the hearts knows what the mind of the Spirit is, because He intercedes for the saints according to the will of God." (NAU Rom. 8:26-27). When we do not know how to pray as we should, the Holy Spirit "helps" us.

Herschel Hobbs once explained to me that the word "helps" in these verses is the Greek word, *sunantilambano*. He said, "It means, 'to come alongside someone to help them lift a load.'" When we do not know how to pray as we should, the Spirit stands on the other side of our prayer burden, reaches down with us, picks our burden up, and helps us lift it up to the Father. He then says, "Father, this is what (your name) is trying to tell you." The Spirit helps us by turning our prayer into one that God will answer!

Praying Scripture

Years ago when I was in college, a friend and I began to memorize Scripture. Soon afterward, I found myself praying those same verses back to God. When I did, there was power and authority in my prayers that I had never known before!

Jesus said in John 15:7, "If you abide in Me, and My words abide in you, ask whatever you wish, and it will be done for you." When Scripture abides in us, our prayers become more effective. God's will is found in His Word. When we pray according to His Word, we pray according to the will of God. God then hears our prayers and answers them (cf. 1 Jn. 5:14-15). When I pray Scripture (rightly interpreted) with a submissive attitude toward His will, God listens and answers my prayers according to His will. Because this subject is so important, I will cover it in more detail in the next chapter.

Praying in Jesus' Name

God is a God of authority. The universe is under His authority. The Psalmist said, "But our God is in the heavens; He does whatever He pleases" (NAU Ps. 115:3). Likewise, Job prayed to the Lord, "I know that You can do all things, and that no purpose of Yours can be thwarted" (NAU Job 42:2).

Jesus commanded His disciples to offer their prayers

to the Father in His name. "Whatever you ask in My name, that will I do, so that the Father may be glorified in the Son. If you ask Me anything in My name, I will do it" (Jn. 14:13). Jesus meant that whatever we ask in His name that is in accordance with God's will, He will grant our request. God is too good a Father to give us anything that is not for His glory and our good. When He said to "ask in (His) name," He was instructing us to offer our prayers based on His authority, not ours.

Satan and the demons certainly understand that authority. When Paul cast an evil spirit out of a fortune teller in Philippi, the Scripture says, "(He) turned and said to the spirit, 'I command you in the name of Jesus Christ to come out of her!' And it came out at that very moment" (NAU Acts 16:18). Notice: first, he spoke to the *spirit*, not the woman; second, he *commanded* the spirit to leave her, rather than merely requesting that it leave her; and third, he commanded her "in the *name* of Jesus Christ." Paul had no authority in the spirit world apart from the authority invested to him in Jesus' name!

When I was nineteen, I was singing in a Christian band. We wanted to purchase a sound system but had no money. I went to a bank to secure a loan. They asked me, "What do you have as collateral?" When I replied, "Nothing," they said, "We cannot loan you the money." As I was leaving, the bank vice president said, "Steve, even though you cannot get a loan on your own, you can get a loan if you can get your father to sign the note with you." I did and we secured the money, bought the sound system, and kept singing for Jesus! I discovered that what I could not get from the bank in my name, I could get in my father's name!

Even so, what we could never receive from the Father in prayer based upon our name, we receive based upon Jesus' name. Because we are blood-bought children of the living God, we are in covenant with Him through Jesus. Though we have no "collateral" in heaven's bank from which to draw, Jesus has all the collateral we need! We are to pray in His name so we can enjoy the benefits of His authority!

A Holy Heart

The Psalmist asked, "Who may ascend into the hill of the LORD? And who may stand in His holy place?" (NAU Ps. 24:3). He then answered his own question by saying, "He who has clean hands and a pure heart, who has not lifted up his soul to falsehood and has not sworn deceitfully. He shall receive a blessing from the LORD and righteousness from the God of his salvation" (NAU Ps. 24:4-5). You and I cannot live sinfully and rebelliously and expect God to hear and answer our prayers. God is holy and He demands that we as His children walk in His holiness.

These verses remind me that anyone who has spiritually "clean hands and a pure heart," actually has been "*cleansed* and *purified*" by Jesus. It is *God* who must do the cleansing and purifying if we are going to be able to pray to Him. Once we have been cleansed and purified from our sin, we will "receive a blessing from the Lord." His blessing follows our cleansing and purification. God is holy. He demands that those who approach Him in prayer be cleansed and made holy by the blood of His Son, Jesus Christ (cf. 1 Pet. 1:18-19).

Sin separates sinful man from God. "Behold, the LORD'S hand is not so short that it cannot save; nor is His ear so dull that it cannot hear. But your iniquities have made a separation between you and your God, and your sins have hidden His face from you so that He does not hear" (^NAU Isa. 59:1-2). As we confess and forsake our sins, God purifies us and makes our prayers acceptable.

A Hungry Heart

My "life's verses" are found in Jeremiah 29. There, God spoke though His prophet and said, "'For I know the plans that I have for you,' declares the LORD, 'plans for welfare and not for calamity to give you a future and a hope. Then you will call upon Me and come and pray to Me, and I will listen to you. You will seek Me and find Me when you search for Me with all your heart. I will be found by you,' declares the LORD" (^NAU Jer. 29:11-14). God wants each of us to pray "with all (our) heart." He loves desperate, passionate prayers. The writer of Hebrews tells us that Jesus prayed this way. "In the days of His flesh, He offered up both prayers and supplications with loud crying and tears to the One able to save Him from death, and He was heard because of His piety" (^NAU Heb. 5:7). Praying is not always to be an exercise in calmness and serenity. Sometimes praying becomes more like birthing a baby – loud, desperate, and messy! No wonder Jesus tells us to pray in private with the doors shut (Matt. 6:6).

When it comes to prayer, God wants more than voluminous verbiage filled with mindless, rote ritual. Jesus said, "And when you are praying, do not use meaningless repetition as the Gentiles do, for they suppose that they will be heard for their many words" (^{NAU} Matt. 6:7). God does not desire phony ritual. He wants a passionate relationship with us. In the words of the Psalmist, "As the deer pants for the water brooks, so my soul pants for You, O God. My soul thirsts for God, for the living God; when shall I come and appear before God?" (^{NAU} Psalm 42:1). God listens to a hungry heart!

A Humble Heart

God demands humility. I heard someone say years ago, "When pride walks in, God walks out." God will not give His praise and glory to any human being (Isa. 42:8). If we had His glory, it would destroy us. It would literally burn us up! Thus, we must approach God in prayer with an attitude of humility.

Isaiah saw the Lord in a vision. He was exalted, sitting on a throne, with His robe filling heaven's temple as the angels sang antiphonally regarding His holiness. Surrounded by flashes of light and clouds of glory, his vision of God became so awesome that Isaiah cried out, "Woe is me!" (cf. Isa. 6:1f). In a similar instance, when the Apostle John saw the resurrected Jesus, "(he) fell at His feet like a dead man" (Rev. 1:17). Both of these men were *humbled* in the presence of Almighty God. The spirit with which we should approach God in prayer must be the spirit of humility and meekness.

The Lord requires us to "walk humbly with (our) God" (Mic. 6:8). He commands us to "clothe ourselves with humility…for God is opposed to the proud, but gives grace to the humble" (1 Pet. 5:5). We are to "humble (ourselves) under the mighty hand of God" (1 Pet. 5:6). God says, "But to this one I will look, to him who is humble and contrite of spirit, and who trembles at My word" (^{NAU} Isa. 66:2).

We should approach God with the respect He is due. Yes, he is our heavenly Father through Jesus Christ. But He is also the holy, exalted, Creator and Sustainer of the universe! He is the All-Powerful, All-Knowing, All-Present God who is from everlasting to everlasting! As the song says, "Angels bow before Him! Heaven and earth adore Him! What a mighty God we serve!" Make sure when you pray that you are little and God is big! Be "little enough" for God to use you in prayer.

Challenge:

Will you take these "helps" and apply them to your prayer life? Will you stay filled with God's Spirit so He can help you as you pray? Will you pray the Word of God (Scripture) so you will be sure to pray the will of God? Will you pray in the authority of Jesus' name? And will you ask God to give you a holy, hungry, humble heart that will cause you to be suitable to approach God's throne of grace in prayer?

For Memory and Meditation:

"Whatever you ask in My name, that will I do, so that the Father may be glorified in the Son. If you ask Me anything in My name, I will do it" (^{NAU} Jn. 14:13).

Praying the Word of God

Nothing will enhance your prayer life like learning to pray Scripture. In this chapter we will focus on why and how we should pray Scripture.

The Bible is the Word of God

The Bible is inspired by God (2 Ti. 3:16). It is therefore a work of God, not merely man. Conservative Christians believe in "verbal plenary" biblical inspiration. "Verbal" means that the *words* (not just the ideas) are inspired. "Plenary" means that *all* the words are inspired. The Bible claims to be and is inerrant (Num. 23:19), thus, it is free from all error. It is infallible (Ps. 119:105) in that it is in and of itself unable to lead a person astray (though some have misinterpreted it and gone astray themselves). The Bible is also authoritative (Matt. 15:3), taking precedence over any non-biblical traditions of men. It is eternal (Isa. 40:8), and its truths and moral standards are universal and timeless. Every word of the Bible *is* truth (Jn. 17:17), which is different from merely "containing the truth." It is perfect (Ps. 19:7) because it comes from a perfect God. And the Bible is Christ-centered (Jn. 5:39-40) because its primary focus is Jesus Christ. The Bible leads non-Christians to salvation in Christ (2 Tim. 3:14-15), facilitates their Christian growth and maturity (2 Tim. 3:16), and equips them for effective Christian service (2 Tim. 3:17). Truly, there is no other book on earth like the Bible, the written Word of God. As children of God, we are commanded to read it (Rev. 1:3), hear it (Rom. 10:17), study it (2 Tim. 2:15), memorize it (Ps. 119:11), meditate on it (Ps. 1:2-3), speak it

(Jer. 23:28-29), obey it (Jam. 1:22), and pray it (Jn. 15:7).

Jesus – Our Example

Jesus actually prayed Scripture while He died for our sins on the cross. He prayed Ps. 22:1 when He said, "My God, My God, why have You forsaken me?" (Matt. 27:46). He also prayed Ps. 31:5 when He prayed, "Father, into Your hands I commit My spirit" (Lk. 23:46). Our Lord understood that when He prayed Scripture, He was praying in accordance with the will of God, which meant that God the Father would hear and answer His prayers (1 Jn. 5:14-15).

How do you pray Scripture?

First, you must rightly interpret a Scripture text, and then you must personalize it in prayer. Some call this "claiming a verse," or "standing on a promise" from God's Word. It is wonderful to read the Bible and sense that God is giving you a specific verse (or verses) to pray as a promise to be claimed in your life. How does this work?

Praying for Children

A great place to start in praying Scripture is with parents. Parents should pray for their children while they are growing up. They should pray Luke 2:52, which says, "And Jesus kept increasing in wisdom and stature, and in favor with God and men." Jesus grew intellectually ("in wisdom"), physically ("in stature"), spiritually ("in favor with God"), and socially ("in favor with man"). My wife and I have claimed this verse for our children since our oldest was born back in 1983. For years we cried out and prayed, "Lord, we pray that Grant, Lindsey, Allison, and Bethany will increase in wisdom, stature, and in favor with God and men." We are now praying and claiming this verse for our grandchildren.

Parents should also pray verses that are applicable in the areas of: salvation (Jn. 16:8; Acts 3:19; Rom. 10:13); spiritual growth and maturity (2 Pet. 3:18); the filling of the Holy Spirit (Lk. 11:13; Eph. 5:18); the fruit of the Spirit (Gal. 5:22-23); moral purity (2 Tim. 2:22); direction/guidance (Ps. 32:8; Prov. 3:5-6; Jam. 1:5); the choice of friends (Prov. 18:24); teaching and training their children in the ways of the Lord (Deut. 6:6-9; Eph. 6:4); and honoring and obeying their parents (Eph. 6:1-3). These verses offered up in effectual praying will have an eternal impact on your children as well as your children's children (Isa. 59:21).

Praying for Your Spouse

Married Christians should pray for their spouse. A husband should pray verses like Eph. 5:25 and 1 Pet. 3:7. He can pray, "Father, I ask You to help me love my wife like Christ loved the church and gave Himself for it (Eph. 5:25). I also pray that I will live with my wife in an understanding way, and grant her honor as a fellow heir of the grace of life so that my prayers will not be hindered (1 Pet. 3:7)." Likewise, you can pray for your wife by saying, "Lord, help (her name) to submit unto me as unto You (Eph. 5:22), and help her to see to it that she respects me" (Eph. 5:33).

Married couples should also pray for each other regarding: God's protection over their marriage and their home (Ps. 91:10-11; 127:1); God's blessings on their finances as they give (Mal. 3:10; Rom. 8:32; Phil 4:19); God's presence to permeate their home (Ps. 16:11); good health

(3 Jn. 2); harmony/unity (Ps. 133:1); guarding meal times for family interaction (Ps. 128); and guidance (Ps. 32:8; Isa. 30:21). It is still true: families and couples who pray together tend to stay together.

Praying for Your Church

Local churches need prayer today more than ever. One of my favorite verses to pray for a church is Acts 9:31, which says, "So the church throughout all Judea and Galilee and Samaria enjoyed peace, being built up; and going on in the fear of the Lord and in the comfort of the Holy Spirit, it continued to increase." This verse gives us five things to pray: that our local church will, "enjoy peace," be "built up", go "on in the fear/reverence of the Lord," go on in "the comfort/power of the Holy Spirit," and that it will "continue to increase." Pray for the churches in your city, county, and region similar to "all Judea, Galilee, and Samaria."

There are many other verses to pray for your church. You can pray for: your church to become a house of prayer (Isa. 56:7; Matt. 21:13); God's Spirit to anoint your worship services (Acts 4:31); your pastor as he devotes himself to prayer and the ministry of the Word (Acts 6:4; 1 Tim. 5:17; 2 Tim. 2:15); every member to be a vibrant, verbal witness for Christ (Matt. 4:19; Acts 1:8); the members of your congregation to discover their spiritual gifts and to use them to build up other believers and glorify God (1 Cor. 12:11); God to raise up laborers to go out and work in the Lord's harvest of souls to be won and discipled (Matt. 9:37-38); all the members to give their tithes so the church's financial needs can be met (Mal. 3:8-12;

Matt. 23:23); and for every member to grow and mature in Christlikeness (2 Pet. 3:18). Churches will be spiritually vibrant and healthy as they move forward on their knees.

Praying for the Salvation of Lost People

The Apostle Paul was arguably the greatest Christian ever to live. One of the traits that made him great was his love for lost people (i.e. non-Christians). He loved them so much that he prayed for them to be saved (Rom. 10:1).

We should follow Paul's example and pray for lost people to come to faith in Christ. We should think about anyone who is a family member, a friend, a co-worker, a classmate, a neighbor, or even a first-time acquaintance who does not know Jesus. Pray for them by name. Paul prayed for individual Christians when he "made mention" of them in prayer (Rom. 1:9), and there is good reason to believe that he prayed similarly by name for non-Christians. We should pray for the Lord to convict them of sin, righteousness, and judgment (Jn. 16:8) so they will come to understand their need for salvation. They must understand that they are sinners who are guilty before a holy God. They do not possess the necessary righteousness to enter into a right relationship with God. The best they can do (i.e. their "righteousness") is comparable to filthy, leprous-stained rags before our holy God (Isa. 64:6). They must see their need for the righteousness of Jesus Christ that comes to a sinner through salvation (Phil. 3:9). They need to understand that when they die they will stand before God in judgment and give an account for their deeds done on earth (Rom. 14:10; Heb. 9:27).

Pray that lost people will hear the Gospel of Jesus

Christ and understand that He died on the cross for their sins, and He then rose from the grave so He could offer them salvation (1 Cor. 15:3-4). Then pray that someone will speak the Gospel to them personally, passionately, and biblically so they can hear, believe, and be saved (Rom. 10:14). And then be willing to be that person who shares with them. If we would simply make a list of people we know who do not know Christ, pray for them and seek to share the Gospel with them, our communities and countries could be evangelized within a relatively short time.

Praying for Revival in Your Nation

God wants us to pray for spiritual awakening. Perhaps the classic verse utilized when praying for revival among God's people is 2 Chron. 7:14, which says, "(If) My people who are called by My name humble themselves and pray and seek My face and turn from their wicked ways, then I will hear from heaven, will forgive their sin and will heal their land." That prayer should be in the heart and on the lips of every believer as he prays for revival in his nation.

We should also pray verses such as these as we pray for revival: That righteousness will exalt (our) nation, and that sin will no longer be a reproach to (our) people (Prov. 14:34); that God will revive His work in our nation in the midst of the years, and in wrath He will remember mercy (Hab. 3:2); that God will revive His people again that they might rejoice in Him (Ps. 85:6); that God's people will repent and return to Him that their sins might be wiped away that times/seasons of refreshing might come to them from the presence of the Lord (Acts 3:19); and that the glory of the Lord will fill the house of the Lord (2 Chronicles 7:1).

If Christians worldwide would pray fervently and faithfully for spiritual awakening, God would hear, and in His perfect timing, He would send an outpouring of His Spirit upon His people that would literally shake their nation for Christ! The spiritual tide of revival is presently not among us. Instead, the tide of revival is "out" just now. But through prayer, God can send a new tide of revival back "in," just as He did in America in the First Great Awakening (1730s & 40s), the Great Prayer Awakening (1850s), and the Jesus' Movement (1960s & 70s).

Challenge:

Praying Scripture will change your prayer life. It will help you pray with more authority. It will help you pray according to the will of God, which is mandatory for God to hear your prayer and answer it (1 Jn. 5:14-15). Will you begin to memorize Scriptures that will enhance your prayers? Nothing will fortify your prayers with the power of God and channel your prayers to be within the will of God more than learning to claim and pray specific verses of Scripture. As you intercede to God for the needs of others and petition God to meet your own needs, abide in Jesus and let His words abide in you. Then ask Him whatever you will, and the Lord will shower His answers upon you and the ones for whom you pray!

For Memory and Meditation:

"If you abide in Me, and My words abide in you, ask whatever you wish, and it will be done for you" ([NAU] Jn. 15:7).

The Power of Praying Together

NAU Matthew 18:19-20 – "Again I say to you, that if two of you agree on earth about anything that they may ask, it shall be done for them by My Father who is in heaven. For where two or three have gathered together in My name, I am there in their midst."

In Matthew 18, Jesus was talking to His disciples about disciplining sinful members of the church. It was in that context that He gave a special word about the power of unity, especially related to prayer. He said that when just two believers agreed together in what they were asking in prayer, it would be granted to them. Of course, the answer was contingent upon whether or not they were praying in accordance with God's will (cf. 1 Jn. 5:14-15). But the point was this – there is power in unity. God promises to send His manifest presence when two or three gather in His name and agree in prayer!

Discovering the Power of a Prayer Partner

When I was in college at Union University, one of my roommates and I began praying over a list of prayer requests for several nights every week. We each put about six requests on the list, and then began to lift them up to the Lord in prayer. That list included some of our fellow students who did not know Christ. We prayed over those requests consistently for an entire semester. It was not long before I befriended one of the young men for whom we were praying. I began sharing the Gospel with him. That spring, Billy Graham held a crusade in Memphis. That

57

student and I attended together and I had the privilege of leading him to faith in Christ at the stadium. I am convinced that God used our prayers to help bring about his conversion. I experienced first-hand the power of having a prayer partner.

That incident was life-changing for me. Since then, I have had many prayer partners. I believe that "spiritual synergy" occurs when two or more people begin to pray passionately in agreement over the same requests.

Magnifying the Power of Our Prayers

Praying together with another believer is similar to the concept of a magnifying glass. Under normal conditions, light passes to a surface without being focused. But when someone uses a magnifying glass and focuses the light and its energy on a specific spot, something powerful happens. That focused light held steadily on one spot of a dry piece of paper can actually burn a hole in it. The magnifying glass harnesses the energy and focuses it until it becomes a potent force.

Praying with a prayer partner works in a similar way. Throughout the Bible there are multiple examples of people praying together in agreement as they ask God to answer their prayers.

Old Testament Examples

A prime Old Testament example of someone who understood the power of having prayer partners was King Jehoshaphat, one of the Godly kings of Judah. A huge army of Judah's age-old enemies, the Edomites and Ammonites, along with the Meunites, marched against

Jehoshaphat and his relatively meager military forces (2 Chron. 20:1-2). Even though he was afraid, Jehoshaphat turned his attention to seek the Lord. He called the people of God together. They began to pray and fast (2 Chron. 20:3-4). All the women, children, and men of Judah joined together and sought the Lord in prayer. As the king concluded a powerful prayer, he spoke these faith-filled words: "O our God, will You not judge them? For we are powerless before this great multitude who are coming against us; nor do we know what to do, but our eyes are on You" (2 Chron. 20:12).

God listened and answered! His Holy Spirit came upon a prophet named Jahaziel who gave this message to God's people: "Thus says the LORD to you, 'Do not fear or be dismayed because of this great multitude, for the battle is not yours but God's. Tomorrow go down against them'" (2 Chron. 20:15-16). Jehoshaphat was convinced that the Lord was fighting on behalf of the people of Judah. He obeyed God's command and placed the Levites in front of Judah's armies. The Levites led the charge against their enemies as they sang, "Give thanks to the LORD, for His lovingkindness is everlasting" (2 Chron. 20:21). God answered that day in a decisive way – "When they began singing and praising, the LORD set ambushes against the sons of Ammon, Moab and Mount Seir, who had come against Judah; so they were routed" (2 Chron. 20:22). Praying in agreement was the key to their victory. They called on God together and "The Lord showed up and showed off!"

Another Old Testament example of the power of united prayer comes from the period of the Exile of God's people. Queen Esther was a Jew. She was afraid to enter the royal throne room of King Ahasuerus, King of Persia, to request his help to stop the plans of wicked Haman who intended to annihilate all the Jews in the land. But Esther called for united prayer and fasting. She told her righteous relative, Mordecai: "Go, assemble all the Jews who are found in Susa, and fast for me; do not eat or drink for three days, night or day. I and my maidens also will fast in the same way. And thus I will go in to the king, which is not according to the law; and if I perish, I perish" (Esther 4:14). God honored their prayer of unity. Not only did Esther not perish, but the Jews in the kingdom were also saved, and the king actually sentenced Haman to be hanged on the very gallows he had prepared for Mordecai! Praying in agreement works!

New Testament Examples

In the New Testament, some of the greatest examples of the power of united prayer come from the Book of Acts. After Jesus ascended back to heaven, the believers had gathered together for prayer in an "upper room" in Jerusalem. For ten days they awaited the coming and empowering of the Holy Spirit. During that time, Jesus' disciples, "All with one mind were continually devoting themselves to prayer, along with the women, and Mary the mother of Jesus, and with His brothers" (Acts 1:14). They also took care of various matters (cf. Acts 2:15-26). But the main thing they did was pray. While they were calling out to God in united prayer, the Holy Spirit fell upon them on the Day of Pentecost (Acts 2:1f). They began to miraculously speak "the glories of God" in the native languages of the Jewish pilgrims who had gathered in Jerusalem from regions all over the world. Peter then preached and 3,000 were saved. It is no coincidence that the Christian church was literally birthed in a prayer meeting. God's house is to be "a house of prayer" (Isaiah 56:7)!

Later in Acts, the Lord healed a lame man through the Apostles, Peter and John, outside of the Temple in Jerusalem. A crowd gathered, Peter preached, and many were saved. But the Jewish religious leaders were jealous. They arrested Peter and John and warned them not to preach or teach anymore in the name of Jesus in Jerusalem. The apostles refused, yet they were soon released. When they left the jail, they called their fellow Christians together and engaged in prayer. In agreement they called upon the Lord to fill them with boldness in witnessing, to grant that people would be physically healed, and that signs and wonders be performed in Jesus' name through them. God heard their united prayer and answered remarkably – "And when they had prayed, the place where they had gathered together was shaken, and they were all filled with the Holy Spirit and began to speak the word of God with boldness…. And with great power the apostles were giving testimony to the resurrection of the Lord Jesus, and abundant grace was upon them all" (Acts 4:31, 33).

Again in Acts, King Herod had the Apostle James killed with a sword and also imprisoned Peter. "Peter was kept in the prison, but prayer for him was being made fervently by the church to God" (Acts 12:5). God answered those prayers by sending an angel to liberate Peter from his prison chains. When Peter went to the Christians who had been praying for his release, they hesitated to believe what had taken place. They joyfully witnessed the power of unified prayer!

God Blesses When We Pray Together

Over the years, I have witnessed similar power. In the summer of 1995, I was frustrated while serving as a pastor in Alabama. I was not tired *of* the ministry, but I was tired *in* the ministry. I began to pray and fast. I asked God to send revival to me and to our church family. Others soon joined me in prayer and fasting. We asked the Lord to do what only He could do. After about a year of intense, united prayer, God's manifest presence filled our church one Sunday morning. That day I obeyed the Lord's prompting to extend a Gospel invitation *before I preached*. People were saved in both services that morning before and after I preached. That night, the sanctuary was packed with our members. Why? Because God showed up! For the next ten years, our church grew exponentially. People were saved, baptized, healed (physically, emotionally, and spiritually), and set free from besetting sins. Our church more than doubled in size, led the state in baptisms, and saw lives changed forever by God's power and for His glory. It all started when people began to agree together in prayer.

Do you have a prayer partner? Are you involved in prayer with other believers with whom you are united spiritually? Are you agreeing with them, asking God to answer specific prayers?

The Power of Praying with Your Spouse

If you are married, you should pray in agreement with your spouse. A husband and wife can become, as my friend, Don Miller, calls them, "God's magnifiers." Throughout your entire marriage, you can pray in agreement for any situation you or your family will face. If you have a financial need, agree together and ask God to provide. If you need wisdom about a decision, agree together and ask God to give you direction. If you have a rebellious child, agree and ask God to bring that child back to Himself and to you. Awesome power comes from the united prayers of a husband and wife. Your children will also learn the immeasurable power of prayer. A marriage and family rooted in united prayer will surely stand the testings of life.

The Power of a Praying Church

Our churches must also be filled with prayers offered up from believers who intercede together for specific requests. The pastor and his staff should join in unison as they bathe the needs of the congregation in prayer. Godly deacons should pray in one accord as they serve the staff and the congregation. Every church member should have at least one prayer partner with whom he regularly offers united prayer requests to the Lord. Churches must learn to pray and agree together in order to experience the power of God. Such united prayer will be all the more necessary as our world grows increasingly dark and sinful before the return of Jesus (1 Pet. 4:7).

Challenge:

Ask the Lord to lead you to someone with whom you can cry out to God in agreement through prayer. Then ask Him to hear and answer your collective requests. If you are married, begin to "magnify" your prayers by praying regularly with your spouse. If you have children, let them join you as you call upon the Lord together in faith. Seek to pray in unison with members of your family and your church. Faithful prayer partners will change your life!

For Memory and Meditation:

"Again I say to you, that if two of you agree on earth about anything that they may ask, it shall be done for them by My Father who is in heaven." (Matt 18:19).

CHAPTER 9

Resources for Enhancing Our Prayer Time

NAU **1 Thessalonians 1:2 – "We give thanks to God always for all of you, making mention of you in our prayers."**

Paul was a man of prayer. Read the Book of Acts and the letters he wrote in the New Testament to the various churches and you will quickly ascertain how much Paul enjoyed talking with God. He prayed constantly for the churches he helped plant throughout the Roman Empire, and also for the people in those churches, interceding to the Father about their various needs.

In Romans 16 we read that Paul sent greetings to no fewer than twenty-five believers who belonged to the Church at Rome. How was Paul able to list all of those names? It is doubtful that he could recall that many names from sheer memory. I believe Paul had lists of names that he used for intercession. I believe these were his prayer lists.

At least three times in his letters, Paul references "making mention" of other believers in his prayers (Eph. 1:16; 1 Thess. 1:2, and Phile. 1:4). It seems logical that Paul was able to "make mention" of many specific names of Christians, as well as praying for the specific needs of the various churches, because he regularly used prayer lists.

Over the years I have had people ask me how it was possible to spend a lengthy time with God in prayer. They have asked, "What is there to pray about that takes more than a few minutes?" What they are really asking is "How can I keep a conversation going with God that is genuine and real?"

Most all of us have experienced the awkwardness of being in a conversation with someone when we ran out of things to talk about. That can really be embarrassing, especially if that "someone" is God! Is it really possible to enjoy protracted, meaningful conversations with God even though we cannot see Him or touch Him as we talk with Him?

In this chapter we will look at two of the best resources I have come across and utilized over the years that have helped keep my own times of prayer vibrant – Prayer Cards and a Prayer Notebook.

Prayer Cards

In the late 1990s, I was speaking at a Student Camp in Georgia. The church I served as pastor was growing by leaps and bounds. I was doing my best just to "keep up" as the leader. For years I had memorized Scriptures. I would write out the verses on blank cards the size of a business card and then commit them to memory. During a break at that camp, I was at my motel room reviewing some old Scripture memory cards. I came across two familiar verses, Philippians 4:6-7, that say, "Be anxious for nothing, but in everything by prayer and supplication with thanksgiving let your requests be made known to God. And the peace of God, which surpasses all comprehension, will guard your hearts and your minds in Christ Jesus." Though I had reviewed those verses many times, that day they spoke to me in a fresh way.

As I meditated on those verses, I sensed the Lord

directing me to take every situation or problem that I was dealing with at church or with my family, and write each of them down on an individual card for prayer. I feverishly wrote those individual requests on about thirty cards. Afterward, I sensed the Lord say, "Now, every day I want you to pray over the requests on each card, stop worrying, and trust Me."

I can still see myself sitting on the back porch of that little motel in North Georgia praying over that first stack of cards. When I finished, I said, "Lord, all of these issues are in Your hands. I've prayed over them the best I know how. I now choose to rest in You. I believe You will be working to answer each prayer. I choose to worry about nothing and instead pray about everything! In Jesus' name, Amen."

When I said, "Amen," I cannot describe the sense of relief that flooded over my spirit. I felt as if a heavy load had just rolled off of me and onto God. Actually, that is exactly what happened! We are told in the Old Testament to, "Cast (our) burden upon the LORD and He will sustain (us); He will never allow the righteous to be shaken" (Ps. 55:22). God also says in the New Testament that we should, "(cast) all (our) anxiety on Him, because He cares for (us)" (1 Pet. 5:7). God can easily handle our problems!

But God was not finished giving me a "Prayer Makeover." He was literally birthing a new prayer resource into my life. The next morning as I read my Bible, I came across several verses that applied to some of the very requests I had written down on the prayer cards. I sensed the Holy Spirit say, "Write these verses on blank cards too, not to memorize, but to pray back to Me." Later that morning when I prayed through my prayer cards again, it was amazing how much power those verses added to my prayer time. I had always prayed the promises that I had memorized, but now I could pray many new promises verbatim because I had them actually written on a prayer card.

One of the practical benefits of prayer cards is their portability. I take a stack of these prayer cards with me virtually everywhere I go. Usually, anywhere you see me, I have a stack of prayer cards close by. I take them with me when I am driving so that instead of listening to the radio, I can pray over my cards. I have redeemed many hours over the years praying that way instead of wasting time on less important things.

I also use my prayer cards on "prayer walks." I enjoy walking, and I enjoy praying, so walking and praying is a natural combination for me. I have walked down busy streets in large cities across the country and around the world praying through my cards. Even though I am actually surrounded by many people, when I take prayer walks it is as though I am alone with the Lord. I have also walked on isolated beaches, around my neighborhood, throughout my house, and around and throughout the church buildings where I have served, praying through stacks of prayer cards.

Prayer cards also help you keep your prayer time fresh. If I feel I am starting to "get into a rut" in my prayer time, I simply swap out the stack of cards that I am us-ing and replace them with another stack containing a completely different set of prayer requests and Scripture promises. If I want to keep praying over the same stack, I simply shuffle the deck of prayer cards to rearrange their order. That one little practice has really helped keep my prayer times vibrant.

For almost two decades now I have used prayer cards in my quiet time, and they have proven to be one of the most amazing resources I have ever used. They have helped keep my prayers fresh by sustaining intimacy, vitality, and variety in my daily conversations with the Lord. With my prayer cards, I never worry about, "What am I going to talk to God about?" Instead, the question becomes, "How will I have enough time today to pray about everything listed on my cards?" I think that is a better problem than not having a clue what you are going to say to God when you try to pray!

Prayer Notebooks

My wife, Donna, has used a prayer notebook for years in her quiet time in the early morning. Her prayer notebooks look pretty much like my prayer cards – they are worn out! That is because she has spent so much time praying over the items she logs into those notebooks.

I recently decided to add some additional variety into my prayer time by following her example and using a prayer notebook in lieu of my prayer cards. I have come to appreciate the use of a notebook as a fresh resource for prayer for several reasons. One of the best things about a prayer notebook is that you can actually place pictures beside the names of someone for whom you are praying, something that is virtually impossible to do with a prayer card. It is hard to describe how looking at a picture of someone when you are lifting them up to the Lord enhances your praying.

When I assembled my first prayer notebook about a year ago, I started by putting three pictures of Donna in the notebook – one of her teaching the Bible, one of her decorating our Christmas tree, and another picture of her smiling at me. Below those three pictures, I listed the various Scripture promises I planned to pray for her. As I began to pray for my wife, I literally started weeping. There was just something sacred and holy about looking at a picture of my "fellow heir of the grace of life" while interceding for her.

The same was true as I prayed for my children, their spouses, our grandchildren, and the other members of Donna's extended family. I also copied pictures from the Internet to help me pray more personally for special leaders like the President of the United States, the Justices of the U.S. Supreme Court, the mayor of Memphis, the members of the Memphis City Council, the presidents of our six Southern Baptist Seminaries, etc. Each picture helped enhance my prayer notebook, at least for me, by causing my prayers to be more intimate and genuine. When I pray for a missionary, a preacher, a politician, or a family member while looking at his/her picture, it is almost like I am lifting them up to Jesus while they are there with me!

Prayer notebooks are also good because they allow you to pray over maps. In my notebook, I have a map of the United States of America. I lay my hands over that map and pray for every state in our country by name. I pray for God to bless the Christians who live in those states, asking God to send revival to them and awakening to their desolate churches.

Prayer notebooks also lend themselves to organization. I record my requests by typing lists using my computer. Then I print the various prayer request pages and punch them with a three-hole punch. I then insert the pages into my notebook using simple dividers for various categories like, "Church, Family, Denomination, Spiritual Warfare, Scripture Promises, Bellevue Baptist Church (my church), Calendar Events, Churches & Pastors, Special Requests, etc. The result is a highly organized, efficient prayer resource!

The prayer notebook is also capable of containing many more prayer requests than a stack of prayer cards. I also enjoy my prayer notebook because it allows me to print the lyrics (not the sheet music) to Christian hymns and songs and use them to worship the Lord. I have said for years that the best prayer book is a Bible, and the next best prayer book is a good hymnal.

Challenge:

When you pray, do you have resources to help you create and categorize prayer requests and Scripture promises to prevent you from running out of things to talk about with God? Why not try one of the two resources mentioned in this chapter? Buy some blank business cards, write out some prayer requests and Scripture promises on them, and begin to pray. Or, buy a notebook and some dividers and print out some prayer lists, and use pictures to enhance them. God can use practical resources like these to help take your prayer life to the next level!

For Memory and Meditation:
"We give thanks to God always for all of you, making mention of you in our prayers" (^{NAU} 1 Thess. 1:2).

The Power of Praying Fervently

NAU Acts 12:5 – "So Peter was kept in the prison, but prayer for him was being made fervently by the church to God."

Churches today should resemble the churches mentioned in the Book of Acts. When we read Acts and then analyze our 21st Century churches, we are forced to ask, "Where is the power of God?" Indeed, why do we see so few people being saved? Why aren't more people healed physically? Why don't we experience demons being cast out of people? Why aren't entire cities coming to Christ as they burn their pagan paraphernalia like the new Christians did in the city of Ephesus (Acts 19)? Why aren't modern-day Christians "turning their world upside down" (Acts 17:6) with the Gospel?

I don't believe the primary problem is in our preaching and singing. For the most part, we preach and sing the same words and in the same way they preached and sang in the First Century. Rather, I'm convinced the difference is in the area of PRAYER! We simply do not pray the way they prayed in the Book of Acts. When they prayed, they prayed FERVENTLY.

Acts 12 is all about fervent prayer. Herod the king had arrested a group of Christians. Two of them were apostles, Peter and James. We should note that several "Herods" are mentioned in the New Testament. The one of which we read in Acts 12 is Herod Agrippa I. He was the grandson of Herod the Great. Emperor Claudius gave Herod Agrippa I all of the territory that his grandfather, Herod the Great, had ruled, including Judea and its capitol, Jerusalem. He was the most beloved Herod of all in the eyes of the Jewish religious leaders, partly because of his disdain for the Christians.

Acts 12 tells us that Herod had James executed "with a sword" (v. 2) which probably means he was beheaded like John the Baptist (Mark 6:27). When the king saw that his actions pleased the Jews, he also arrested Peter, the leader of the apostles. Herod held Peter in prison until after the Passover celebration. Afterward, he planned to bring Peter out and execute him as well.

At that point, we read these wonderful words: "Peter was in prison, but prayer for him was being made fervently by the church to God." We need to appreciate the contrast intended by the writer: "Peter was in prison, *but prayer*... (emphasis mine)." The prayers prayed for Peter were far from being casual or routine. Instead, they were urgent, desperate, and fervent prayers. The Greek word translated "fervently" in Acts 12:5 is *ektenos*. It means to pray "eagerly; fervently; constantly." "Fervent" prayers rise from a boiling, passionate heart that pleads with God and must have an answer! It's the kind of prayer Jacob offered when he wrestled with the Angel of the Lord (the preincarnate Jesus): "I will not let you go unless you bless me" (Genesis 32:26). God loves it when His children pray with such fervency!

The fact is, Jesus prayed with fervency. When He was in the Garden of Gethsemane, just before He was arrested, Luke tells us, "And being in agony He was praying very fervently; and His sweat became like drops of blood, falling down upon the ground" (Luke 22:44). The writer of Hebrews referenced that same occasion with these words: "In the days of His flesh, He offered up both prayers and supplications with loud crying and tears to the One able to save Him from death, and He was heard because of His piety" (Hebrews 5:7).

Jesus poured out His heart in passionate, fervent prayer to His Father, just like His followers did later in Acts 12 on behalf of Peter. The Father answered Jesus, and He also answered those who interceded for Peter.

What happens when we pray fervently?

God Provides His Peace (Acts 12:1-6)

When the early Christians prayed fervently, Peter experienced and enjoyed a supernatural peace. The Bible says, "On the very night when Herod was about to bring him forward, Peter was sleeping between two soldiers, bound with two chains, and guards in front of the door were watching over the prison" (Acts 12:6). Just a few hours from being executed by Herod's soldiers, wearing chains and positioned between two soldiers, Peter rested like a baby.

Only God can give such peace. Jesus said to His disciples in John 14:27, "Peace I leave with you; *My peace* (emphasis mine) I give to you; not as the world gives do I give to you. Do not let your heart be troubled, nor let it be fearful." Jesus displayed "(His) peace" in the back of the boat when everyone else was panicking because of the storm-tossed sea (Matthew 8:24). That is the same peace that Peter experienced. And it is a result of fervent prayer.

God commands us to, "Be anxious for nothing, but in everything by prayer and supplication with thanksgiving let your requests be made known to God. And the peace of God, which surpasses all comprehension, will guard your hearts and your minds in Christ Jesus" (Philippians 4:6-7). When we pray fervently, anxiety exits because God's peace has entered!

But there is another result of fervent prayer to be considered.

God Activates His Angels (Acts 12:7-11)

When you and I pray, God dispatches His angels on our behalf. They minister to us and also to those for whom we pray. While Peter was fast asleep, the Christians were praying. God sent one angel to free him from prison (Acts 12:7f). Peter's chains fell off supernaturally, the angel led him out to safety, and then the angel humbly disappeared.

In the Old Testament, Daniel was thrown into the lion's den because the king's servants, who were jealous of righteous Daniel, made it illegal for him to pray to God. When the king, who loved Daniel, came to see if Daniel's God was able to deliver him from the lions, Daniel shouted triumphantly: "My God sent His angel and shut the lions' mouths and they have not harmed me, inasmuch as I was found innocent before Him; and also toward you, O king, I have committed no crime" (Daniel 6:22). One angel, dispatched by God, because of Daniel's and the king's prayers, "shut the mouths of lions" (Hebrews 11:33).

The Bible is replete with examples of how the prayers of God's people activated angels. They even came to minister to Jesus after He prayed and fasted in the wilderness. "Then the devil left Him; and behold, angels came and began to minister to Him" (Matthew 4:11). Notice that they came *after* Jesus prayed. The angels were the answer to His prayer!

The author of Hebrews also indicates that angels are assigned to help us as well: "Are not all angels ministering spirits sent to serve those who will inherit salvation?" ([NIV] Hebrews 1:14).

We need the protection of God's angels and we receive it when we pray fervently.

But something else happens when we pray fervently.

God Surprises His Servants (Acts 12:12-17)

When Peter came to himself and understood that what had happened to him was not a dream, he ran to the very place where the believers had gathered to intercede for him. When Peter knocked at the door, a servant girl named Rhoda answered. Upon hearing Peter's voice, she left him outside the door and ran to tell the others the joyous news. But they didn't believe her! Meanwhile, Peter kept knocking until they finally let him in. When at last they saw him, they were amazed. Peter told them to report what had happened to James, the senior pastor at Jerusalem, and also to the rest of the brethren there. Then Peter left to go to another place before Herod discovered he was missing.

Both Peter and the people praying for him were shocked at what God had done. They had prayed fervently asking God to work miraculously, and that is exactly what He did. Yet, they were so surprised when they saw Peter, they did not really know what to do or say!

That's what God still will do when His people pray fervently. He not only answers our prayers, but He does so in amazing, abundant ways. God is not limited in power. He is able and willing to open the windows of heaven to pour out bountiful blessings on His children when they call on Him fervently in prayer.

When Jesus fed thousands of people with the lunch of a young lad, the Bible says in Matthew 14:19-20: "Ordering the people to sit down on the grass, He took the five loaves and the two fish, and looking up toward heaven, He blessed the food, and breaking the loaves He gave them to the disciples, and the disciples gave them to the crowds, and they all ate and were satisfied. They picked up what was left over of the broken pieces, twelve full baskets." Jesus blessed them abundantly! There were twelve baskets filled with left over fragments of food so that each of the apostles could have his own basket to remind him that with God nothing is impossible!

Jesus promised similar "abundance" when He said in John 10:10, "The thief comes only to steal and kill and destroy; I came that they may have life, and have it abundantly." Jesus came to give us "life on a higher plane." Dr. Roy Fish used to call it, "Life with a plus!"

That is what we experience when we engage God in fervent, passionate prayer! Paul confirms this in ^{KJV} Ephesians 3:20-21 – "Now unto him that is able to do exceeding abundantly above all that we ask or think, according to the power that worketh in us, unto him be glory in the church by Christ Jesus throughout all ages, world without end. Amen."

If your brand of Christianity is "boring" compared to what you read about in the Book of Acts, start praying fervently! God makes us abundantly joyful when we become

His house of prayer (Isaiah 56:7). When we pray fervently, God surprises His servants.

God Vindicates His People (18-25)

When Herod's soldiers woke up, Peter was gone! Assured that the soldiers had conspired against him, Herod had them executed. He then traveled from Jerusalem to Caesarea. He was angry with the people from the coastal towns of Tyre and Sidon just north of Caesarea. Because they were dependent on Herod for food, the leaders of those cities came and sought to appease his anger. It was then that Herod donned his regal garments and made a speech. The delegates from Tyre and Sidon praised him crying out continually, "The voice of a god and not of a man!" (Acts 12:22).

While Herod enjoyed the praise they gave him, God didn't. God dispatched yet another angel, this time to strike down Herod because "he did not give God the glory, and he was eaten by worms and died" (Acts 12:23). Read the text carefully. It does not say that he died and was eaten by worms. Instead, the worms ate him and he died. It was a gruesome end for a wicked man.

Luke then contrasts Herod's death with these words: "But the word of the Lord continued to grow and to be multiplied. And Barnabas and Saul returned from Jerusalem when they had fulfilled their mission, taking along with them John, who was also called Mark" (vv. 24-25).

God punished Herod Agrippa I, vindicated James, and rescued Peter, all because God's people prayed fervently.

That is the power of fervent prayer!

Challenge:

How desperate are you for God to answer your prayer? Can you say with Jacob, "I will not let you go unless you bless me"? Are you willing to not allow God to rest until He moves in your situation? Will you plead passionately, violently, desperately with God in fervent prayer? When we pray like that, God is moved – and that is when He moves on our behalf.

For Memory and Meditation:

"So Peter was kept in the prison, but prayer for him was being made fervently by the church to God" (Acts 12:5).

Praying for the Sick

NAU James 5:14-16 – "Is anyone among you sick? Then he must call for the elders of the church and they are to pray over him, anointing him with oil in the name of the Lord; and the prayer offered in faith will restore the one who is sick, and the Lord will raise him up, and if he has committed sins, they will be forgiven him. Therefore, confess your sins to one another, and pray for one another so that you may be healed. The effective prayer of a righteous man can accomplish much."

Should Christians pray for people to be healed? Does God still heal people today like He did in biblical times? Is it wrong to go to a physician? Does taking medicine indicate a lack of faith? If a Christian dies from disease, is it because he did not have enough faith to be healed?

Hard questions.

For over thirty years in the ministry, I have been asked these and other difficult questions like them. I have stood at the bedside weeping and praying alongside a husband as he held his dying wife's hand. Even though many Godly people had prayed for the Lord to heal her, she died. Why? Does God still heal? If so, why didn't He?

Hard questions.

I once met a preacher who claimed that God promised perfect health to all Christians who would just believe. I listened to him preach and then talked to him after he finished. I asked him if he really believed what he said, why was he wearing glasses? He had no answer.

The first time I grappled with praying for the sick, I

81

was a twenty-six year old pastor. At that time (1984), I was in seminary. In one of my seminary classes we had studied the verses above from James regarding healing. I learned that some theologians believe that the "oil" mentioned in James 5:14 referred to First Century medicine, similar to the oil and wine used by the "good Samaritan" to heal the wounds of the man who'd been beaten and robbed (cf. Luke 10:34). To me, that seemed like a convenient cop out. I sided with the commentators who said "oil" in that text referred to anointing oil used symbolically to invoke the power of the Holy Spirit.

One Wednesday night at a prayer meeting, the topic of healing came up. As church members shared prayer requests, I noticed that most of their requests were about people who were physically ill. I asked a question that shocked them: "How should we pray for these sick people?" They stared at me and asked, "What do you mean?" I then said, "Let's consider our options: 1) We can ask God to heal them by a miracle alone; 2) We can ask God to heal them by medicine alone; 3) We can ask God to use both medicine and miracle to heal them; or 4) We can ask God to help them be as pain-free as possible until they die. Which should we choose?"

I then read James 5:16 aloud. I refer to it as the "Catholic, Charismatic, Baptist verse." It includes three phrases. Catholics tend to emphasize the first phrase: "Therefore, confess your sins to one another." Charismatics tend to emphasize the second phrase: "Pray for one another so that you may be healed." Baptists seem to prefer the last phrase: "The effective prayer of a righteous man can accomplish much." I told them that the entire verse is important, and that we must never split it up to emphasize the part we like and ignore the parts we don't.

I became convinced that God wants us to pray for people to be healed. I also believe that we should use every medical help accessible in order to be healed.

In His providence, God does not always heal the way we desire. No one can demand or decree that God must heal someone. We are not God. There is a holy tension regarding this matter of praying for people to be healed. But it is a good tension that I believe is biblical.

I have prayed in faith for people to be healed, and yet they died. I have also prayed for people to be healed, not necessarily sensing that my faith level was "high," and yet God healed them. Such secrets "belong to the LORD" (Deuteronomy 29:29).

Most people I have seen healed over the years were those who prayed for healing and also utilized physicians and medicine. Yet on several occasions I have seen God miraculously heal people in ways that defied all odds with no medicine involved. I cannot explain why or how it happened. I can only say that I have witnessed it personally.

I am eternally indebted to a woman I have never met. Decades ago when my mother was twenty-four years old, she was diagnosed with breast cancer. The doctors had already removed one of her breasts, and they were scheduled to remove the other. Mother was in a hospital room semi-conscious due to medication. The night before her second mastectomy was scheduled, her hospital roommate, an older woman who herself was recovering from a recent mastectomy, climbed into my mother's bed, put mother's head in her lap, and prayed all night for God to heal her. When the doctors came in the next morning, mother's cancer was totally gone! God had healed her. When my mother became fully conscious, that sweet lady shared the Gospel with her and led her to Jesus. She then told my mother, "When you get back to Kentucky, find a good Baptist church, tell the preacher you've been saved, get baptized, and begin to grow as a Christian."

Mother returned to Central City, Kentucky and was baptized. My father was soon saved and baptized as well. That is how and why I grew up in a Baptist Church, was saved, and called to preach. A woman I hope to meet one day in heaven prayed and asked God to heal my mother. Mother was fond of saying, "I lost a breast, but I gained a Savior, and it was worth it!"

Does God still heal? Yes! In Exodus 15:26, God referred to Himself as "the LORD who heals" (Hebrew – "Yahweh-Rapha"). Since God is "Jehovah-Rapha," what does the Bible teach about healing?

Reasons for Physical Sickness

Sickness originated as a result of the sin of Adam and Eve. Theologians refer to it as "The Fall" (cf. Genesis 3:1f). Extreme pain was added to childbirth, toil was added to man's labor, and disease and death were introduced to bring about the inevitable end of bodily life.

Interestingly, some of the sicknesses among us today are direct consequences of our personal sins. God has decreed that we will reap what we sow. If we sow to the flesh (i.e. live sinful, disobedient lives), we will reap disease, decay, and death from our sinful natures (cf. Galatians 6:7-8). Thus, if someone smokes and develops lung cancer, his sin is to blame. If someone commits gluttony and develops diabetes, his sin is to blame. If someone is sexually immoral and contracts HIV or some other STD, his sin is to blame. Sin can cause disease.

The Bible also teaches that Satan and demons can cause some disease (certainly not all). When Jesus cast a demon out of a mute man, the mute man began to talk (Matthew 9:32-33). Jesus also healed a woman with "a sickness caused by a spirit" (KJV- "a spirit of infirmity"; Greek - *pneuma asthenias*). For eighteen years that evil spirit had caused her to be bent double. But when Jesus cast out the demon, she was healed (Luke 13:11).

The Bible goes on to say that diseases also occur for the works of God to be displayed (John 9:1-3); for God's glory to be manifested in healing (John 11:4); for God to test an individual (2 Corinthians 12:7-10); for God to discipline an individual (Numbers 12); and for God to take a person home to heaven (2 Kings 13:14).

Some Principles Regarding Healing

It seems clear that God wants us to pray for people to be healed physically. There is really no other way to interpret James 5:14-16 which plainly says, "Pray for one another so that you may be healed." Yet, it also seems clear in Scripture that not everyone we pray for will be healed.

Even a spiritual giant like the Apostle Paul received a negative answer from God when he asked for physical healing. Three times Paul prayed and asked God to remove his "thorn in the flesh," which was actually caused by "a messenger (Gr. *angelos*) of Satan." Each time God answered, "No." God seemed to be saying, "Paul, you're a better man with this illness than without it. You need My all-sufficient grace more than you need physical healing" (cf. 2 Corinthians 12:7f). That's not a cop out – that is Scripture.

Scripture also teaches that God wants us to utilize doctors. Jesus Himself validated the ministry of medical physicians when He said, "It is not those who are healthy who need a physician, but those who are sick" (Matthew 9:12). However, we must never rely exclusively on doctors and medicine. In the Old Testament, there was a king of Judah named Asa who did just that. In the thirty-ninth year of his reign, Asa developed a severe foot disease. He sought help only from his physicians without also asking God to heal him. Consequently, God allowed him to die (2 Chronicles 16:12f). Asa should have looked to God for healing first, and then to the physicians.

Herein, I believe, is the biblical "sweet spot" where we should live and minister regarding praying for the sick. We should pray for people to be healed, but we should also seek medical care from physicians.

In 2000, I was diagnosed with an autoimmune disease called Myasthenia Gravis (severe muscular weakness). I have had major surgery, I take medicine every day, and I see doctors regularly. But I also pray daily that God will heal me. I ask God to allow me to be symptom free and medicine free before I die. I pray in faith for healing. But I also take my medicine, and then leave it with the Lord.

All people for whom we pray will not be healed, just like all people to whom we witness will not be saved. But more people get saved in churches that preach the Gospel and invite people to receive salvation in Christ than in churches that don't. And more people will be healed physically in churches that pray for people to be healed than in churches that don't.

God Wants to Heal Our Entire Being

In 1 Thessalonians 5:23, Paul said, "Now may the God of peace Himself sanctify you entirely; and may your spirit and soul and body be preserved complete, without blame at the coming of our Lord Jesus Christ." Every person consists of three parts – spirit, soul, and body. God wants to heal every part of us. He heals our spirit when we become a Christian at regeneration (2 Corinthians 5:17). He heals our soul through the process of sanctification as the Holy Spirit transforms us daily into Christ's likeness (Romans 12:2; 2 Peter 3:18). At times God heals our bodies from sickness while we are on earth. But our ultimate physical healing will occur at our glorification when Jesus returns, and our bodies will then be raised imperishable. We will then enter heaven, never to die again (1 Corinthians 15:50f; Revelation 21:3-4)!

Challenge:

Do you pray for people to be healed? If not, why not? The Bible says you should pray and ask God to heal people. Encourage them to go to the doctor and take medicine as well, but encourage them to trust God ultimately. Regardless of what happens, give God praise.

For Memory and Meditation:

"Therefore, confess your sins to one another, and pray

for one another so that you may be healed. The effective prayer of a righteous man can accomplish much" (James 5:16).

The Sinner's Prayer – Asking Jesus into Your Heart

Romans 10:9-10, 13 - That if you confess with your mouth Jesus as Lord, and believe in your heart that God raised Him from the dead, you will be saved; for with the heart a person believes, resulting in righteousness, and with the mouth he confesses, resulting in salvation.... for "WHOEVER WILL CALL ON THE NAME OF THE LORD WILL BE SAVED."

According to our text, and others like it, the Bible validates the appropriateness of praying and confessing with your *mouth* and calling on the name of the Lord Jesus from your *heart* for salvation.

When a lost sinner calls on Jesus through a prayer of repentance and faith, God sends His Holy Spirit to dwell eternally in that person's heart. The indwelling Spirit is actually Christ in that person (Galatians 4:6). God adopts him and the Spirit of His Son, Jesus, indwells his heart, causing him to cry out, "Abba, Father!"

Because God commands all people everywhere to repent (Acts 17:30), desires for all people everywhere to be saved (1 Timothy 2:3-4), and does not desire for anyone to perish (2 Peter 3:9), anyone can be saved. Because Jesus died for the sins of everyone in the whole world (1 John 2:2), His atoning sacrifice causes all people to be potentially "savable."

According to Romans 10:9-10, 13, praying as one confesses with his mouth and believes with his heart is synonymous with, "asking Jesus into your heart." Yet, some complain that the phrases, "asking Jesus into your heart" or "inviting Christ into your life," are not found in Scripture. According to them, we should not utilize them in evangelism.

That is a "straw man" argument. While it is true that those exact phrases do not appear in the New Testament, the truths do appear. That's also the case for phrases like "biblical inerrancy" and "the Trinity." While those exact words are not in the Bible either, the truths are.

Theologian Wayne Grudem validates the use of a sinner's prayer. Veteran pastors such as Charles Spurgeon and John MacArthur have also utilized a sinner's prayer at the end of their sermons to help non-Christian listeners believe in Christ.

Some object that many have prayed such a prayer, but in time, their lack of perseverance indicated that obviously they were not genuinely converted to Christ. Without question, someone can pray a sinner's prayer and either not understand what is at stake or not be sincere. If that happens, praying a sinner's prayer will do that person absolutely no good. Mindlessly mouthing the words of a sinner's prayer is NOT a magical method of attaining salvation. However, all people must call upon the name of the Lord in order to be saved.

Many who pray to receive Christ at an early age actually experience legitimate conversion. But because they do not experience sufficient follow up and discipleship, they are hindered in their spiritual growth. Nevertheless, poor discipleship practices do NOT indicate that calling upon the name of the Lord via a sinner's prayer is either invalid or unscriptural.

Even when the Bible simply tells us to "Believe," and we do so, that kind of believing involves a prayer in the sense that there must be a turning to God, a yielding of oneself to God, a surrendering of the will toward Him. While prayer does not have to be verbalized, we must respond to God by calling out to Him in repentant, faith-filled prayer, in order to be saved.

You can mindlessly and meaninglessly pray a sinner's prayer and not get saved, but you cannot get saved without responding to God in prayer, calling on Jesus!

Let's focus on at least three issues:

God Desires to Transform Our Sinful Hearts

In the Old Testament, God predicted He would change the hearts of repentant, faith-filled men. The New Covenant would be superior to the Old Covenant. The Law promised that after Israel would break the commandments and be cursed, God would circumcise their hearts. Deuteronomy 30:6 says, "And the Lord your God will circumcise your heart and the heart of your offspring, so that you will love the Lord your God with all your heart and with all your soul, that you may live."

Jeremiah built on this as the basis for the New Covenant. Stressing the relationship between the Law and the human heart, he wrote, "Circumcise yourselves to the LORD and remove the foreskins of your heart" (Jeremiah 4:4). He also said, "For this is the covenant that I will make with the house of Israel after those days, declares the Lord: I will put my law within them, and I will write it on their hearts. And I will be their God, and they shall be my people" (Jeremiah 31:33).

Ezekiel also promised a future heart-work performed by God for His people. The Spirit Himself would indwell them. He said in Ezekiel 36:26–27, "And I will give you a new heart, and a new spirit I will put within you. And I will remove the heart of stone from your flesh and give you a heart of flesh. And I will put my Spirit within you, and cause you to walk in my statutes and be careful to obey my rules."

The New Testament writers continued to expand on this concept. Paul said in Romans 2:28-29, "For he is not a Jew who is one outwardly, nor is circumcision that which is outward in the flesh. [29] But he is a Jew who is one inwardly; and circumcision is that which is of the heart, by the Spirit, not by the letter; and his praise is not from men, but from God."

Paul also affirmed that Christ resides in the hearts of Christians. He said in Colossians 3:15, "Let the peace of Christ rule in your hearts…." Likewise, Peter admonished in 1 Peter 3:15, "But sanctify Christ as Lord in your hearts."

In the Old Testament, God promised to do something new by transforming the hearts of men and women who repented of their sin and placed their faith in God's Messiah. In the New Testament, God fulfilled that promise.

God Desires to Indwell Individuals with His Holy Spirit

The indwelling Spirit within a believer is a major New Testament theme. Jesus said, "Even the Spirit of truth, whom the world cannot receive, because it neither sees Him nor knows Him. You know Him, for He dwells with you and will be in you" (John 14:17). Paul also said, "You, however, are not in the flesh but in the Spirit, if in fact the

Spirit of God dwells in you. Anyone who does not have the Spirit of Christ does not belong to him" (Romans 8:9).

When the Holy Spirit came upon Mary, she was overshadowed with the power of the Most High God. Jesus literally, physically came into her body (Luke 1:31f). Today, whenever a person is saved, the Spirit also "comes upon" that person spiritually (Acts 1:8), baptizes that person into Christ, and causes that person to partake and drink of Himself (the Holy Spirit) (1 Corinthians 12:13). Just as Christ was birthed physically in the womb of Mary when the Holy Spirit came upon her, even so He is birthed spiritually in the heart of every believer whenever the Holy Spirit comes upon him at conversion.

No wonder Paul could say in Colossians 1:27, "Christ in you (is) the hope of glory," and in Ephesians 3:16-17, "That He would grant you, according to the riches of His glory, to be strengthened with power through His Spirit in the inner man (i.e. the heart), [17] so that Christ may dwell in your hearts through faith."

God desires to indwell individuals with His Holy Spirit.

God Desires for People to Be Saved

What must transpire for a person to be saved?

We must be exposed to the *Gospel*. Romans 10:13-14 says, "For 'WHOEVER WILL CALL ON THE NAME OF THE LORD WILL BE SAVED.' [14] How then will they call on Him in whom they have not believed? How will they believe in Him whom they have not heard? And how will they hear without a preacher?"

No one can be saved until they have access to the Gospel of Jesus. Ephesians 1:13 says, "In Him, you also, after listening to the message of truth, the gospel of your salvation – having also believed, you were sealed in Him with the Holy Spirit of promise." Here we see the Biblical "Ordo Salutis" – "The order of salvation." 1) We hear the truth/the Gospel; 2) We believe; and 3) We are sealed in and saved by Jesus through the Holy Spirit.

We must *repent* of sin. Jesus said, "Unless you repent, you will all likewise perish" (Luke 13:3). Paul told his listeners, "Therefore repent and return, so that your sins may be wiped away, in order that times of refreshing may come from the presence of the Lord; [20] and that He may send Jesus, the Christ appointed for you" (Acts 3:19). To repent is to do a spiritual U-Turn. One turns away from his wicked ways and then turns to God.

We must *believe* in Jesus. In His first sermon, Jesus said, "Repent and believe in the gospel" (Mark 1:15). We must believe in our hearts that Jesus died for our sins and rose from the dead. We must place our faith and trust in what Jesus has done to secure our salvation. We are saved by and justified through faith in Jesus (Ephesians 2:8; Romans 5:1).

We must *receive* Jesus as Lord and Savior. The Bible says, "But as many as received Him, to them He gave the right to become children of God, even to those who believe in His name" (John 1:12). The word "receive" is the Greek word *lambano*, which means, "to accept as true, receive, take hold of, seize, choose, select." The concept of "receiving and accepting Jesus" is found throughout John's writings (John 7:39; 12:48; 13:20; 14:17; 20:22).

We must *call* on Jesus' name in prayer. Calling on the name of the Lord is prayer! And any sinner can pray for salvation!

Soon after Cain murdered his brother Abel, we read, "Then men began to call upon the name of the LORD" (Genesis 4:26). That obviously refers to prayer. Others like Abraham (Genesis 12:8), Moses (Exodus 34:5), David (1 Kings 18:24), Elijah (1 Kings 18:24), Isaiah (Isaiah 55:6-7), Hosea (Hosea 14:1-2), Joel (Joel 2:32), Peter (Acts 2:21), Paul (Romans 10:13), Ananias (Acts 22:16), either called on God in prayer, or encouraged others to do so.

What is "praying a sinner's prayer" for salvation if it is not "calling on the name of the LORD"?

While we all agree that no exact wording of a sinner's prayer is prescribed in Scripture, and there is no official sinner's prayer, yet, a heart-felt sinner's prayer is still a valid, scriptural truth that assists people as they call on Jesus' name and RESPOND to the Gospel!

The thief on the cross (Luke 23:42), the former blind man (John 9:35-38), and the repentant tax collector (Luke 18:13), didn't all pray the same words, but they all "believed in their hearts" and "confessed Jesus with their mouths." Consequently, they were all saved!

When a sinner repents, believes, and receives Jesus, calling on His name in prayer for salvation, Jesus regenerates that person and comes to dwell in his heart through the Holy Spirit. With that understanding, the phrase "asking Jesus to come and live in your heart" is indeed a biblical truth.

In fact, the phrase "Invite Jesus into Your Heart," just might be one of the best ways of articulating the fundamental difference between the Old and New Covenants.

Challenge:

Have you ever repented of your sin, believed in and received Jesus, calling on His name through a sinner's prayer to ask Him to come live in your heart through His indwelling Holy Spirit? If not, why not do that today? Ask those in your class to share when they prayed and asked Jesus into their hearts as well. Make sure everyone in your class has genuinely been saved.

For Memory and Meditation:

"For 'WHOEVER WILL CALL ON THE NAME OF THE LORD WILL BE SAVED'" (Romans 10:13).

HOW TO BECOME A CHRISTIAN

1. God knows you and loves you.

"For God so loved the world, that He gave His only begotten Son, that whoever believes in Him shall not perish, but have eternal life" (John 3:16).

2. You are a sinner.

• **Sin is breaking God's laws** - "Everyone who practices sin also practices lawlessness; and sin is lawlessness" (1 John 3:4).
• **Everyone has sinned** - "For all have sinned and fall short of the glory of God" (Romans 3:23).
• **The punishment for sin is spiritual death and separation from God** - "For the wages of sin is death" (Romans 6:23). "But your iniquities have made a separation between you and your God" (Isaiah 59:2).

3. Jesus died on the cross to pay the penalty for your sins.

"But God demonstrates His own love toward us, in that while we were yet sinners, Christ died for us" (Romans 5:8).

"For Christ also died for sins once for all, *the* just for *the* unjust, so that He might bring us to God, having been put to death in the flesh, but made alive in the spirit" (1 Peter 3:18).

4. You Must Repent, Believe, and Receive.

• **Repent of your sin.** Turn from your sin and turn to God - "Repent therefore and return, that your sins may be wiped away" (Acts 3:19).
• **Believe in Jesus.** Believe that Jesus died for you and rose from the dead to save you from sin - "That if you confess with your

mouth Jesus *as* Lord, and believe in your heart that God raised Him from the dead, you will be saved" (Romans 10:9).

• **Receive Jesus.** Call on His name and accept/receive Him as your Lord and Savior - "Whoever will call upon the name of the LORD will be saved" (Romans 10:13).

5. You can Repent, Believe, and Receive RIGHT NOW by calling on Jesus in a prayer like this...

Dear Jesus, thank You that You love me. I know that I am a sinner. I have willfully broken your laws, and I deserve to be punished. But I thank You that You allowed Yourself to be punished for my sins when You died on the cross. I believe that You died on the cross and rose from the dead to save me. I repent and turn from my sin. I put all of my faith and trust in You. I call on You and ask You to save me right now, Lord Jesus. Wash me by Your blood, and fill me with Your Holy Spirit. I receive You as my Lord and Savior. Thank You for saving me! In Jesus' name, Amen!

Signed _____

Date _____

If you repented of your sin, believed in Jesus, and called on His name to save you, you have become a Christian! Now, find a good Christ-honoring, Bible-believing church near you to grow in grace as you read the Bible, pray, and fellowship with other believers.

Free teaching guides
for all non-disposable curricula
for 12- or 13-week study
are available at auxanopress.com

Non-Disposable Curriculum

- Study the Bible and build a Christian library!
- Designed for use in any small group.
- Affordable, biblically based, and life oriented.
- Free teaching helps and administrative materials online.
- Choose your own material and stop/start time.

Audio-commentary material for teachers by the author at additional cost.

Available Now

Core Convictions: Confidence About What You Believe
When people have confidence about what they believe, they are more inclined to make daily decisions from a Biblical perspective. *Core Convictions* has the potential to educate the average person in the pew with the core essentials of classical Biblical theology. Ken Hemphill

Connected Community: Becoming Family Through Church
The need for community is universal. Only the church can deliver authentic community that will last forever. This study explores the mystery of God's eternal plan to reveal His manifold wisdom through the Church. Ken Hemphill

God's Redemption Story: Old Testament Survey
Explores the story line of the Old Testament by focusing on twelve key events in the life of Israel and linking them together to provide a unified view of God's redemptive work in history. Ken Hemphill

The King and His Community: New Testament Survey
This study begins with the birth of Jesus and ends with Him walking among the seven churches of the book of Revelation. It covers twelve key passages that tell the story of the King and the worldwide spread of His church. Kie Bowman